SENSORCISES™

Skyhorse Publishing books may be purchased in bulk at special discounts for sales promotion, corporate gifts, fund-raising, or educational purposes. Special editions can also be created to specifications. For details, contact the Special Sales Department, Skyhorse Publishing, 307 West 36th Street, 11th Floor, New York, NY 10018 or info@skyhorsepublishing.com.

Skyhorse® and Skyhorse Publishing® are registered trademarks of Skyhorse Publishing, Inc.®, a Delaware corporation.

Visit our website at www.skyhorsepublishing.com.

10 9 8 7 6 5 4 3 2 1

Library of Congress Cataloging-in-Publication Data is available on file.

Print ISBN: 978-1-62914-747-5
Ebook ISBN: 978-1-63220-121-8

Printed in the United States of America

SENSORCISES™

Active Enrichment for the Out-of-Step Learner

Laurie Glazener

Foreword by Eric Jensen

Skyhorse Publishing

Table of Contents

Table of Contents

About the Author

Laurie Glazener is a Title I Reading Coordinator with an Administrative license in Springfield, Oregon. She has taught in the resource room, the classroom and Title I programs. She completed her Bachelor and Masters degrees at the University of Oregon; in 2002 she began work on a doctorate in Educational Leadership at the College of Education, University of Oregon. Her outstanding achievements include developing and implementing a highly successful Kindergarten phonemic awareness program that consistently meets the national standards for performance; leading staff efforts in school reform by providing trainings and model teaching in the classrooms; and recently developing and implementing a physical education warm-up program based on exercises used by occupational, sensory integration and visual therapists. She frequently presents to educational professionals at the local, state and regional levels. Glazener was nominated to appear in *Who's Who in American Education* in 2001, 2002 and 2003; she is also a board member of the Brain Center, a non-profit organization devoted to using brain-based interventions to prevent violence in youth.

Foreword by Eric Jensen

Many teachers unknowingly perceive academic and behavior problems as students merely being mischievous. But there's usually much more to it than evil intent. Often, teachers are witnessing symptoms of poorly developed neural circuitry that can be changed for the better. Improper, ineffective or missing neural connections between the body and brain often lie at the heart of difficult classroom behavior. Rather than a lack of intelligence, flawed character, laziness or willful disobedience, the underlying cause may be a student's need to "rewire" the system. Understanding this concept is the first step toward helping these students become better learners. Understanding the enormous plasticity of the human brain, particularly in the early years, is the vital next step. This creates a supreme opportunity for intervention and success.

This visually appealing book is a handbook of carefully chosen sensory exercises for any teacher or parent who desires to help those students who are slightly "out of step" with their classmates—but not to the degree that they have been identified for extra resources or serious intervention. Fortunately, *Sensorcises*™ also benefits every other learner in the classroom. We've all been students before—think of how uncomfortable it can be to sit still in your chair listening to a long lecture! Even the most interesting topic can tire your brain. If only teachers were in the habit of stopping for a moment to let everyone refresh themselves... how much more enjoyable would learning be! Sensorcises make great transitions between subjects or activities, they boost energy levels, require little or no preparation and are a lot of fun to perform. Every student in your class will relish the chance to stand up and perfect them.

But this book is more than just a catalog of activities. I think you'll find that it as fascinating to read as it is a joy to look at. Each chapter is full of up-to-date scholarly research and information about the neuromotor dysfunctions that seem to be more and more prevalent in schools today. The REAL system—Relax, Energize, Activate and Lead—is mapped out step by step so you'll have no trouble learning to use it. Accompanying photographs show you exactly how to perform every Sensorcise. The last chapter of the book will teach you how to design your own sensory transitions for specific academic subjects. There are also lists of activities that expand on the *Sensorcises* theme for you to incorporate into your regular curriculum and lesson planning.

I am excited by the launch of a product that is completely dedicated to exploring and enhancing the union of the brain and body. I have certainly learned much from the author's wealth of knowledge about sensory dysfunction and its solutions. I hope you will, too. Enjoy the ride!

1 Introduction to Sensorcises

Acquiring knowledge and applying what we know is the process of learning. Basic learning happens in three stages: experiencing an event through our sensory systems, cognitively assimilating the incoming information and responding to the event in some meaningful way. The brain constantly uses this process to develop new skills and generate a more complex understanding of the world.

Under this model, learning and behavior challenges are rooted in at least three possible sources of neural dysfunction: the sensory input system may be underdeveloped or dysfunctional, the processing system within the brain may not be working optimally or the motor output system is off-kilter for some reason. Fortunately, because the brain is flexible and able to learn new ways of processing information, educators can still meet the needs of children in the classroom.

As educators, we are charged to keep all students learning and achieving high academic performance standards. This sounds simple enough until you look at the range of learners in most classrooms today. You may find students who speak some language other than English as their primary language at home; students from families that are abusive; hungry children; students with undetected learning challenges or who have the symptoms but do not qualify for special help; and talented or gifted children who deserve to be learning at a higher level of knowledge and application but for whom you have no time to create lesson plans or activities. The diversity of learners and increased personal accountability for meeting standards has left many teachers wondering how they can accomplish everything. It might help if you had an idea of where learning can go wrong. Let's take a look at the development of the brain and the process of developing skills.

Neural Plasticity and Learning

brain cells (neurons)

dendrites

At the brain cell level, learning looks like this: Our body encounters some physical sensation, which causes some neurons (brain cells) to create connections (dendrites) with other neurons so that they can communicate with each other about it. The more often they communicate, the faster they process information. Neuronal groups form patterns of communication called pathways that with repeated use become channels through which cells can easily act upon demand. Neural plasticity is the ability of the brain to change in response to new demands or sensations from the environment. Basically, if some skill is learned incorrectly, a new skill pathway can be initiated and developed in order to learn it correctly. Although the process for replacing old pathways with new ones is easy to describe—attentive repetition and practice—it is not necessarily easy to do. But however formidable, keeping a child motivated to try new techniques during numerous practice sessions is well worth the challenge in the long run. The implications of neural plasticity and its effects on improved learning are far-reaching.

Sensory Activation and Learning

Sensory integration is the process of receiving sensory input and then organizing, interpreting and using this information to make a motor response. Movement is complex. For children to be able to sit in a chair and write their name, they must first have the voluntary postural control for sitting without support from their hands and the finger-clasping skills to hold a pencil. These foundational motor skills needed for school are developed in the first few years of life as a child interacts with the environment. The skills first manifest in a series of primitive reflexes and postural responses and eventually become the coordination required for voluntary movement. But why so much concern with sensory activation and dysfunction now? What is different about students today? Are there more sensory-related problems than there used to be? What observations can we make about being a child in this day and age that might partially explain the sensory processing abilities of today's students?

Children are spending far less time on the floor and on their stomachs than they did in the past. The new car seats that double as infant chairs contribute to infants being left in the seats for longer periods of time—it was once more convenient for parents to remove a child from the car seat to bring him into the house than it was to bring the car seat into the house. Once out of the car seat, the baby would be held by his parents or placed on the floor, getting a chance to explore the environment on his stomach and develop a sound base for motor development. The motor functions developed by "tummy time" can be learned no other way. (Concurrently, the recommendation to put babies on their backs to sleep has led some people to mistakenly conclude that babies should *always* be placed on their backs.) Toddlers and young students who once resourcefully devised their own construction toys and building blocks for making forts and doll houses now have prefabricated materials to play with. Weeding the garden, baking cookies, decorating sock puppets and helping with chores are all traditional activities that have been replaced by more convenient methods for doing them, or have vanished from some homes entirely (there are fewer gardens and more prepackaged food, for example). Finally, games that require physical manipulation of materials, like checkers and *Monopoly*, are not as common as their computer and video game counterparts and alternatives.

The joy of childhood is the opportunity to continuously explore life through every sensory modality, making as many connections in the brain as possible. Ideally, each child would spend hours upon hours exploring and experimenting with their environment and developing the neural networks needed to do such things as walk, reach and grasp, sit still and move the eyes from left to right without having to focus any conscious thought at all on the task. Children who miss this opportunity to learn about the world and perfect their sensory and motor abilities begin school with very significant disadvantages. Teachers anticipate that children will enter their classroom already able to perform four basic sensory motor tasks automatically: sit still, pay attention, hold a pencil and follow a line of print with their eyes. These are reasonable expectations and yet we all know students (and some adults) who struggle with one or more of these production control skills. So what happened to prevent the task from reaching an automatic level in the brain? A look at brain development may provide some insight.

Residual Reflexes

To ensure survival immediately after birth, primitive reflexes operate until more mature reflexes and sensory systems develop and take over the function of the survival reflex. Postural control reflexes prepare a child for advanced movement patterns such as creeping, sitting or rolling. Both primitive and postural reflexes help create myelinated pathways (insulated connections between brain cells that turn ordinary neural pathways into cerebral super-highways) to and from the sensory processing systems. Myelination increases the speed of neural processing, thereby improving the brain's capacity for executive function (Frederick, 1998).

Many of these original reflexes are eventually replaced by intentional movements. Students with learning or behavior problems, however, commonly have residual primitive reflexes left over from their infanthood and react to the environment involuntarily; sometimes they also appear to have movement problems (Cheatum & Hammond, 2000). Intentional movement patterns never fully emerge in these children and they remain at the mercy of involuntary physical responses. But what prevents these reflexes from developing into intentional movements? The cause is not always clear. Birth trauma, limited amounts of tummy time as an infant and organic differences in the brain are all possible culprits. If a primitive reflex is retained beyond six to twelve months of life, it is aberrant and can affect the development of the gross motor skills, fine motor skills and the particular sensory system with which the reflex is associated. Retained reflexes can be readily observed as movement problems, like extreme clumsiness, for example.

Evidence suggests that behavioral, cognitive and even academic problems can often be explained as problems with production control (sensory-motor responses) rather than as deficits in knowledge (Houde, 2000). The brains of people diagnosed with attentional disorders show differences in the functioning of the motor and attentional areas of the brain (Zametkin, 1995). Interference with normal processing occurs when a non-threatening stimulus is perceived as a threat and the brain stem response takes over the situation. Once the "fight or flight" impulse has been activated, higher levels of brain involvement are not immediately attainable. Fortunately, there is evidence that motor activities can improve sensory functioning (Kermoian & Campos, 1988; Yan et al., 1998) and academic learning (Gilbert, 1977). Any simple muscle movement will stimulate the growth of axons (Changeux, 1997), but a coordinated series of movements will actually create myelinated connections at a more rapid rate (Brink, 1995; Sunbeck, 1996).

What does this mean for students? It is never too late to build a better brain. Thanks to neural plasticity, we can help students strengthen their ability to process sensory information. Teachers are in a position to assist with this transformation and Sensorcises can help.

What Are Sensorcises™?

Sensorcises are treatment exercises adapted from those used by occupational therapists, speech pathologists, audiologists, developmental optometrists, neuro-developmental specialists and several prominent researchers in the brain-based learning community. Each exercise was selected for inclusion based on the following standards:

- The duration of the activity is brief enough to fit into a tiny window of time during or between lessons.
- The activity requires very little space and minimal or no preparation of materials.
- The activity requires no special equipment.
- The activity can be performed by the whole group yet still be effective for the individual participant.

The task of helping individuals develop strong neural pathways through movement has traditionally been relegated to occupational, physical, visual, auditory processing and sensory integration therapists. In all of these disciplines, treatment exercises utilize the brain and body connection to assist a patient. A growing body of brain research, however, supports other specific teaching and learning approaches that benefit the most skilled and most troubled learners simultaneously. These approaches, sometimes known as brain-based learning strategies, incorporate neurological discoveries into lesson design and teaching methodologies in the classroom. Several available resources can help teachers create optimal learning environments, devise differentiated assignments for the diverse population of learners in the classroom and employ beneficial teaching strategies to enhance a learner's ability to apply new knowledge in practical situations. *Sensorcises* represents just one instructional technique that utilizes scientific knowledge to strengthen the relationship between the brain-body connection and learning. Of the thousand or so sensory activities reviewed for inclusion in this book, only about forty of them met all these criteria.

How Will Sensorcises Help You in the Classroom?

Sensorcises help students develop the very basic sensory skills they need to learn. The many resources available through special education programs are usually reserved for only the most severely challenged students. A great frustration of many educators is the knowledge that a student needs some kind of help but is not deficient enough to qualify for extra assistance. Sensorcises are designed for that student.

After I was introduced to the concept of sensory development and integration and took time to reflect upon my students' performance within that framework, I made some (surprisingly) obvious discoveries. My problem students were not lazy; they just did not have the physical skills needed to sit still, pay attention, hold a pencil or track a line of print across a page. These production control skills were skills I could certainly help them develop, right within the classroom during my regular teaching schedule! (If a student is busy trying to keep her body from falling out of her chair, chances are even my most entertaining lesson will not keep her attention.) Instead of developing new pathways for learning, some students are mentally preoccupied with things like postural control or visual tracking ability. I was amazed to find that after just a few short weeks of practicing this program, my students began to make small improvements in their reading speed and story recall. Off-task wiggling was far less frequent and my students continued to noticeably improve throughout the year.

Of course, not every academic challenge will vanish by adding an exercise or two to your day—there is no substitute for good instruction—but Sensorcises help build a better foundation for receiving, interpreting and applying instruction to learning tasks. They do not take away from academic instruction; they just replace the natural confusion during transitions and idle time during lessons with purposeful movement aimed at improving sensory processing skills. I think you will be pleasantly surprised by the positive outcomes of including these exercises throughout the day.

The REAL Way to Optimize Learning

The REAL way to optimize learning is to increase the speed at which we process the information that comes in from the senses and respond to it via the motor system. Each Sensorcise will do one of four things: relax the retained reflexive responses of the brain, increase the cells' ability to send and receive electrical messages, create better connections between the two sides of the brain and activate or strengthen the sensory skills needed to master a production-related skill. Relax, energize, activate and lead into academic instruction—REAL sequences for real learning.

Relax

Relax exercises calm us mentally and physically by mechanically shifting the activation of neurons from the back of the brain to the front. When we are in tense situations, our bodies respond with primitive "fight or flight" responses from the brain stem region of the brain. And the brain stem is interested in only one thing—survival. Once the brain stem is given the danger signal, it sends chemical messages to the muscles and tendons to prepare for an immediate response; your breathing quickens, your tendons contract and your muscles tense up. The chemical messengers, cortisol and epinephrine (adrenaline), remain in the system long after the stressful event has occurred. Many stressed-out students in our classrooms will respond well to an opportunity to relax their survival response. The more relaxed our tendons are, the better we are able to comprehend the information coming our way. Stretching and lengthening activities help us move from the brain stem response area to the frontal lobes, where reasoning and problem-solving occur.

Energize Cellular Communication

Energize exercises assist with communication between the sensory cells throughout our body. Electrical currents, which can be sensed by imaging equipment or wavelength reading apparatus, carry messages through the central nervous system from cell to cell all the way to the brain for processing, and then back out through the nervous system with messages from the brain indicating what movement or action to take. The body's circuitry can become clogged or sluggish if the cells are not prepared to send and receive these electrical charges. Proper hydration and well-oxygenated blood flow promotes better electrical conductivity of cells. An overworked messaging system is inefficient for completing learning tasks. We can help keep electricity flowing freely through our body by staying hydrated and unblocking pathways with specific blood flow and oxygen stimulating exercises.

Activate Large Muscles for Optimal Learning

Activate exercises activate communication between the two hemispheres of the brain and stimulate the balancing system. The sensory systems responsible for balancing are the visual processing system, the vestibular (inner ear) system and the proprioceptive and muscle cell communication system, which work together to alert us to our relationship to gravity, or our location in space relative to other people and things. We rely upon these systems to plan, organize and complete any series of movements that are directed toward a purpose. Our brain's two hemispheres perform different but related functions. By activating communication between the right and left hemispheres, we generate more myelinated connections and are able to switch lobes with greater flexibility when solving problems.

Lead "Sense"-ibly

Lead exercises provide a transition between *Relax, Energize* and *Activate* exercises and the academic task at hand. As with the previous exercises, *Lead* activities help learning by activating the systems needed during an upcoming activity and by strengthening the sensory pathways needed for performing a specific task. This is the final step of physically preparing brain cells for optimal cellular communication. In other words, the brain and body are now able to work together efficiently to receive and apply new concepts from the curriculum. But it is not enough to be ready at only the physical level; leading "sense"-ibly will also prepare the mind for learning by tying previous academic material to the upcoming lesson. Taking time to activate prior knowledge and warm up the sensory system readies the brain, body and mind for learning.

How to Use this Book

Chapters 2 through 5 of this book explain each segment of the REAL technique; the final chapter brings them all together. *Relax, Energize, Activate* and *Lead* contain not only descriptions of activities you can use, but also background on the science and research that support their effectiveness. Each activity is thoroughly described and illustrated with photographs for your ease of use and immediate comprehension. Whether you want to relax students' chest and shoulder muscles before a writing activity or expend some of their extra energy before an assembly, you can design a REAL sequence by choosing one activity from each chapter and presenting them in order to prepare all your students for the classroom learning or other school event that follows.

The final chapter, *Getting Started*, provides examples of REAL activity sequences and possible scripts for you to use when you introduce them to your students. The appendix is full of additional activities that address the needs of learners with sensory dysfunction; all of these extra activities can be performed using materials you already have at your school and in your classroom. A complete bibliography and a list of books and publications that address these issues will help you further your own knowledge of this field.

If children can sit, stand and walk, we mistakenly take for granted that they have the sensory motor skills needed to function in school and everyday activities. School success requires a much more sophisticated series of sensory abilities than originally believed. These activities were gathered and organized to assist you with teaching the advanced sensory skills needed for learning.

2 Relax

What the Research Says...

About Stress...

Stress induces poor memory, fuzzy thinking and a lack of creativity by causing nerve cells to lose dendritic branches and spines, reducing their ability to transmit information to each other. The high levels of cortisol sustained by prolonged stress shrink the hippocampus, thereby impacting the body's production of new neurons and negatively influencing your emotional responses to any situation (Diorio et al., 1993; Howard, 2000; Kempermann, 1999; Sapolsky, 1996; Sylwester, 1995). Furthermore, the adrenaline response associated with stress reinforces the body's primary physical defenses by diverting blood flow to the brain to increase the blood flow to the heart, lungs and large muscles (Diorio et al., 1993), negatively impacting the brain's ability to think critically or solve problems.

About Breathing

Brain cells have a higher rate of metabolism than any other cell type in our body, which causes the brain to consume more oxygen than any other organ. Although it contributes to only two percent of the body's weight, it uses 20 percent of the body's oxygen (Greenfield, 1996)! Breathing exercises can enhance oxygen flow, reduce heart rate, and anxiety (Bernardi et al., 2000), and provide the brain with the fuel it needs to facilitate new learning. Approximately two-thirds of the cells that transmit oxygen to the blood stream are located in the bottom third of the lungs; deep breathing brings oxygen directly to those cells and maintains an oxygenated blood flow to the brain (Jensen, 2000a).

An ideally functioning breathing system will automatically (and appropriately) adjust itself to meet physiological demands. However, some people have an overactive startle response and hold their breath during stressful events. In others, stress too easily triggers their "fight or flight" response system, causing their breathing to become shallow, their heart rate to increase, and blood to flow from their brain to the large muscles. Anger, fear, and frustration can trigger similar responses, as well. Consciously taking deep breaths from your diaphragm helps interrupt any involuntary breathing responses you may display and restore your body's normal breathing patterns (Sapolsky, 1996).

About Stretching

Another one of the body's reactions to stress is to contract muscles and tendons, which can cause physical pain if they contract too often. Lengthening (stretching) the muscles has been found to relax the stress response of the muscles and tendons (Hannaford, 1995). Specifically, the over-contraction of muscles in the lower back reduces the flow of cerebrospinal fluid. Stretching releases the contraction of the muscles, thus allowing this fluid carrying messages through the central nervous system to the brain to flow more freely

(Promislow, 2000). Taking a quick break from a lesson in order to stretch the back and body has the added benefit of reducing the strain that sitting puts on the musculoskeletal system (Henning et al., 1997). The yoga practice of clearing the mind of chatter by focusing on breathing and the sensation of holding the stretching postures may even increase the concentration and cognitive abilities of participants immediately following the exercises (Dash & Telles, 1999).

What the Research Means

Who can benefit from *Relax* exercises? Stiff Stan, who cannot turn his neck and moves his whole body instead; Tina and Tyrell Toe-Walkers, who find it difficult to walk heel-to-toe; and Henry and Haruko Hyper-Vigilant, who cannot keep their attention on anything and who are easily distracted. These students all exhibit symptoms of a super-stressed or survival-oriented physiology.

Symptoms of stress include:
- hyper-vigilance
- dilated pupils
- quickened breathing
- muscular contraction
- increased heart rate

When the body reacts to a high-stress situation, instinct demands that it be ready to do whatever it takes to survive. This is a useful response when it's time to duck out of the way of a speeding bus or fight off a dangerous animal. However, if for some reason the body chemically responds to a difficult math problem in the same way, instinct is no longer serving the body's needs. The performance of simple physical activities seems to change the physiology of the stress response by interrupting the stress reaction of the brain stem and allowing more complex cognitive processing to take over—enabling students to snap out of a survival mode and into a problem-solving mode.

Transitioning to Relax Exercises

Hint: Whenever you move into an activity, describe and demonstrate it simultaneously. Limit your directions to one or two steps at a time to enable you to do so. For example, try this introduction to the activity, *Fly Free*:

"It looks like we need to get some of our kinks out. Everyone, please stand up and stretch for a second. Okay. Now, let's prepare our upper body for writing. Put both arms up in the air, reaching as high as you can." (You reach your arms up in the air.) "Now, reach across your head with one arm and gently hold the elbow of your opposite arm." (You reach across your head and hold your elbow.) "Let's take a deep breath together." (Exaggerate your own breath so everyone can see and follow along.) "Take another breath" (breathe again) "and again" (breath again). "Now, switch arms...." (You switch arms, et cetera.)

Modeling an exercise not only helps ensure that students properly perform it but also lessens any confusion for those who do not follow oral directions well.

Activities

Fly Free

Purpose of this Activity:

The chest, arm and shoulder muscles control most of the movements and postures that a student uses at school. The continued use of these muscles causes them to shorten in response to fatigue and tension. *Fly Free* lengthens the muscles of the upper chest and shoulders. Stretching these muscles helps them relax and function with less effort during handwriting activities. The same stretch also works to improve other fine motor skills, such as those used for manipulating equipment (like scissors) or typing on computer keyboards.

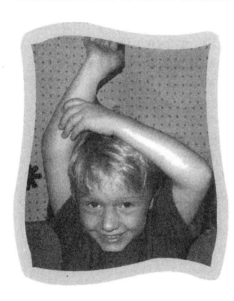

What to Do:

1. Raise both arms above your head.
2. Reach one arm across the top of your head and gently hold the elbow of the other (straight) arm.
3. Take three to five deep breaths.
4. Switch arms.

Push Through Barriers

Purpose of this Activity:
The tendon guard reflex is an automatic, stress-triggered process that shortens the calf muscles and locks the back of the knees in instinctive preparation for the body to stand and run from danger. The gastroc-

nemius muscles (associated with the Achilles tendon) and the soleus muscles contract in the calf while antagonistic muscles in the shin relax, shifting movement to the toes. In order to maintain balance and adjust to the new, forward-thrusting posture, the muscles in the back and neck tense to reduce the mobility of the spine (and, in the process, hamper the flow of cerebrospinal fluid.) Not only does this fluid move from the central nervous system through the brain carrying nutrients, hormones and neurotransmitters and removing toxins, it also helps keep the brain cool (Promislow, 2000). *Push Through Barriers* relaxes the tension in the constricted back muscles, removing the partial obstruction of the flow of the cerebrospinal fluid (Hannaford, 2002).

What to Do:
1. Stand and place your hands on the back of a chair or against a wall.
2. Slide one foot back twenty inches and lean forward.
3. Inhale.
4. Bend the knee of your forward leg while keeping the back leg straight. Lift the heel of the back leg off the floor.
5. Push the heel towards the floor three times while exhaling.
6. Switch legs and repeat.

Desk Breathing

Purpose of this Activity:
One aspect of the body's stress response is the tensing of posterior muscles (the muscles in the back of the body and limbs). When this tension is released, the brain becomes balanced and emotional and mental stress responses no longer interfere with its ability to reason and solve problems. If you have ever placed your head on a desk, sighed and slowly stretched back to an upright position, you have already performed a version of this activity.

What to Do:
1. Lay your head on a desk and exhale.
2. Breathe in and slowly extend your head and neck as you sit up.
3. Gently exhale and place your chin on your chest.
4. Inhale while slowly raising your chin off the chest as high as possible without straining the neck muscles.
5. Exhale and bring your head to its natural position.

Release Pressure Points

Purpose of this Activity:

Emotional stress can weaken front neck muscles. In response, the muscles in the back of the upper body overcompensate by contracting too hard in order to maintain a posture—potentially causing a tension headache. Symptoms of these headaches can be reduced by massaging the acupuncture points associated with the carotid artery, which causes analgesic neurotransmitters to fire off. These analgesic transmitters (the body's pain-relieving chemicals) are thought to be partially responsible for the relief from symptoms patients experience after acupuncture treatments.

What to Do:

To ease symptoms caused by tension in the legs, shoulder or neck, breathe deeply and massage the points on the body as described below. If an area is sore, rub it until the soreness is eliminated. Massage all three places or just one spot to help reduce the effects of stress on your body and mind.

1. *Back Points*—the two points on the left and right where the neck meets the skull. Massage them until pain is gone. You'll know you when you find them; they are tender if you have a headache.
2. *Front Points*—the two points on the left and right beneath your collarbone, halfway between the shoulder and your neck in the collarbone's natural hollow.
3. *Leg Points*—the two points on the outside of each leg. You can find them by standing with your hands at your sides. They are the lowest and most tender places on the thighs.

Lighten the Brain Stem's Heavy Load

Purpose of this Activity:
Stress primarily manifests itself in the neck. Releasing neck muscle tension frees the body of other symptoms related to stress. Many of us do some version of this exercise instinctively.

What to Do:
1. Relax your arms naturally at your sides. Gently let your left ear fall toward your left shoulder. Stop when you feel muscle tightness.

2. Put your right arm behind your back and breathe deeply. Hold this position for thirty seconds. Repeat on the other side.
3. Finish by gently dropping your head to the chest and smoothly rolling it in a semi-circle. *Never roll your neck completely around!* You have many very fine nerve endings in the back of the neck that can be pinched or damaged if you force your head to roll in a circle.

The Brain Wiggle

Purpose of this Activity:

Cerebrospinal fluid is the electrical messaging conductor that integrates the brain and the body and carries cellular waste out of the brain and into the blood. The sacrum (tailbone), because of its triangular shape and location at the

base of the spine, is said to be one of the "pumps" for this fluid. As the sacrum moves along with your body's natural movements, it moves the fluid along the spine. The efficiency of this process is reduced when the vertebrae around the tailbone area are fixed in place instead of loose and relaxed. If you notice that your students are in strained postures or engaged in a great deal of off-task wiggling, they are most likely trying to loosen their vertebrae after sitting for longer than is comfortable. *The Brain Wiggle* is designed to release the tension around the tailbone by massaging the hamstring and gluteus muscles in a gentle way.

What to Do:

1. Sit on the floor with your hands behind your hips and your fingertips pointing forward.
2. Gently lift your feet off the floor.
3. Rock back and forth on your tailbone and rotate in small circles to release the tension in one hip and then the other.

Variation:

Perform this activity while sitting in a chair.

Seated Toe Touches

Purpose of this Activity:
Maintaining balance and using gravity instead of muscles to move your body will help release tension in the hips and pelvis and make sitting more comfortable (Bjorklund & Brown, 1998).

What to Do:
1. Sit comfortably and cross one foot over the other at the ankles.
2. Reach forward with your arms, allowing gravity to pull your head down into your lap as far as it will go.
3. Inhale.
4. Exhale and reach for your toes three times.
5. Change legs.

Variations:
1. Perform this activity with your eyes closed.
2. Perform this activity standing up, taking care not to lock your knees.

Stretch the Jaw Joint

Purpose of this Activity:
Opening your mouth wide is an instinctive act that brings fresh oxygen to the brain, gets rid of excess carbon dioxide and relaxes jaw muscles. There are more nerve endings in

the jaw joint than in any other joint. In fact, more than fifty percent of the neurological connections between the body and the brain pass through the area of the jaw joint! We tend to tighten our jaw when we concentrate too hard or are under stress. Releasing tension in this area will help relax your entire body (Gold, 2002; Howard, 2000).

What to Do:
This is a noisy, stress-releasing activity. Have fun!
1. Pretend to yawn.
2. Put your fingertips against any tight spots you feel on the jaws.
3. Make a deep, relaxed, yawning sound while stroking away your tension. Begin at the chin and gently stroke along the jaw line up to your earlobes, temples and across your forehead (above the eyebrows). Increase the pressure of the stroking movement by as much as you can tolerate.

3 Energize Cellular Communication

What the Research Says...

About the Body Electric...

Without proper hydration and electrolyte balance, communication between your cells is compromised. Electrolytes are the positively or negatively charged ions—charges in the electrical system that ignite a cell's production of neurotransmitters and other chemical messengers (Restak, 1995)—that we get from the sodium, potassium and chlorine in our diets. Water is the solvent that dissolves these ions so nerve cells can use their charge to create a smooth current of electrical communication. At the cellular level, all brain activity depends upon tiny electrical impulses sparked by the movement of electrolytes in and out of a cell. These rapid, tiny impulses profoundly affect our ability to learn, remember, feel, think and physically act in our lives (Tortora & Anagnostakos, 1990). Symptoms of electrolyte imbalance can be as mild as slight mental disorientation and heart rate irregularities or as severe as cardiac arrest and possibly death.

Water is essential to other cellular functions, as well. The lymphatic system that helps remove toxins from cells relies on water to transport waste. Water also aids oxygen distribution to the brain and body by keeping the surface of the air sacs in the lungs moist, enabling the oxygen to dissolve and move into the blood (Howard, 2000). The carotid artery, the first artery leaving the heart, sends freshly oxygenated blood directly to the brain. Staying hydrated keeps your blood oxygen at optimal levels and reduces your personal stress (Hannaford, 1995).

About Heart Rate Variance...

In addition to efficiently pumping blood through the entire body, the heart also functions as the body's electrical power plant, generating *forty to sixty times* more electrical power than the brain does. Heart health is often determined by using pulse and blood pressure measurements to calculate the number of heartbeats per second (heart rate). A more sophisticated way of determining heart rate is with an electrocardiogram (an EKG), which shows the normally occurring, beat-to-beat changes in heart rate (heart rate variability, or HRV).

When the heart rate variance is uniform (coherent), the para-sympathetic nervous system—assisted by the amygdala—synchronizes with the heart, resulting in even breathing patterns and pulse rates. This produces a coherent brainwave pattern in the basal part of the frontal lobes (the prefrontal cortex) and the neocortex areas associated with finding patterns, which allows the thalamus to take in information from the senses. Heart rate coherence is part of maintaining an optimal learning state. In contrast, if the HRV pattern is non-coherent, the amygdala, presuming danger, sends messages to the sympathetic nervous system, which floods the body with stress hormones and creates an incoherent brainwave pattern in the prefrontal cortex and neocortex. As a result, the thalamus ignores any sensory information not directly related to survival (Hannaford, 2002) and learning can neither continue nor begin.

Scientists recently found that the electrical pulses of cells stabilize themselves into evenly spaced wave patterns following exercises designed to bring about heart rate coherence (stabilized and predictable HRV patterns) (McCraty et al., 2001). Studies indicate that certain breathing exercises can enhance oxygen flow and assist in reducing heart rate and anxiety (Bernardi et al., 2000; McCraty et al., 1995).

About Pressure Points...

Acupuncture and acupressure points are areas of sensitivity located in more than two thousand places on the body. Rubbing or inserting needles at these points stimulate various sensory receptors that transmit impulses to the hypothalamic-pituitary system at the base of the brain. This region of the brain produces endorphins, the body's natural analgesics (Omi, 1998). When we experience symptoms of discomfort while working on a task, two desires compete in the brain: manage the pain (survival related) and attend to the task at hand (not survival related). Survival always wins (Greenfield, 1996). In studies involving productivity and pain management, workers who took breaks to manage discomfort regularly increased their productivity (Henning et al., 1997).

What the Research Means

Primitive reflexes—like the sucking reflex, which causes infants to suck on anything that is placed in their mouth, or the Moro reflex, which causes infants to throw out their arms as if to brace themselves when they are startled or encounter the sensation of falling—function to ensure an immediate response to the environment outside of the womb. As an infant grows, the postural and equilibrium reflexes (including the amphibian and segmental rolling reflexes, precursors to the ability to crawl) replace involuntary reactions to stimuli and set the stage for intentional reactions. These reflexes assist with development of the motor control systems needed for walking, crawling, creeping, sitting and standing (Cheatum & Hammond, 2000). If the necessary nerve-connecting pathways do not fully mature before movement-related reflexes and purposeful movements arise (perhaps because a child spent more time in an exerciser than her body needed and less time playing on her stomach, which would have developed those pathways), a child may retain the primitive reflexes. Schoolwork puts demands on the sensory-motor system that require intentional response; reflex retention may lead to social, emotional or academic problems (Goddard, 2002).

So which students may have retained one or more primitive reflexes from their first few weeks of life? Who are the students that would benefit from a chance to "plug in" their electrical system? Angry Andre, who cannot control his emotions and is still fuming from losing his soccer game at recess (unable to shift focus). Social Sophia, who focuses on everyone else and their problems, relying on her peers to model the behavior expected of her but getting distracted by their social interactions and failing to notice the academic behaviors she originally set out to mimic (poor adaptability to classroom change). Jumpy Jamal, who is easily startled by sudden noises that his classmates are able to ignore (hyperactive startle response).

Symptoms of retained reflexes include:
- hypersensitivity to sensory stimulation like noise, light, smell or touch
- inability to shift focus
- difficulty with the catching and hitting skills needed for ball games
- poor adaptability to change; reliance on peers to model expected behavior but an inability to filter out essential academic behaviors from superfluous social ones

- auditory confusion and trouble ignoring background noise
- poor manual dexterity and handwriting skills
- difficulty with visual tracking
- speech impediments
- inability to sit still
- poor balance
- poor posture

Transitioning to *Energize* Exercises

By encouraging students to stay hydrated, teaching them to control their heart rhythms and helping them manage physical discomfort with techniques associated with acupuncture, teachers can help students keep electrical communication flowing freely (Greenfield, 1996). Good electrical communication within the central nervous system maps new neural pathways over any retained reflex patterns to make them more efficient.

Hint: The first two activities in this section, *Drink Water* and *Heart Smart*, set the foundation for maintaining the connection between the body and the brain; both exercises should be performed repeatedly throughout the day.

Hint: Explaining the reasons for performing these exercises is just as important as telling students how to do them. For example, try this introduction to the activity, *Heart Smart*:

"Let's make sure our body's electrical system is up and running. Take a drink of water and a few deep breaths before we begin. Now, place your hand over your heart and imagine that you are breathing from that part of your chest."

Hint: Energize activities are essential to creating a *calm* learning environment. This may sound like a contradiction but in reality is not. These activities clear the electrical circuits in the body. Overloaded circuits block the normal flow of electrical current to the brain and cause stress. Activities that reconnect our electrical system lead to calmer and more relaxed states.

Hint: In addition to incorporating at least one *Energize* activity into your daily routine, use these exercises whenever your group seems frazzled or fragmented.

Activities

Drink Water

Materials Needed:
Lots of water and plenty of opportunity to drink it

Purpose of this Activity:
Water is an instant brain booster. Drinking water increases energy, improves concentration and enhances mental and physical coordination—all things that benefit your students as they learn material or apply new skills and ideas in a variety of ways.

What to Do:
Build drink breaks into your schedule whenever possible and allow students to keep bottles of water at their desks.

Note:
More water may mean more requests to go to the bathroom. Just remember that the benefits of hydration to learning by far outweigh the drawbacks of a student's absence from class for a few minutes.

Heart Smart

Purpose of this Activity:

Variations in heart rate intervals correspond to variations in brain wave activity. When your heart beats irregularly—

perhaps during moments of anger, frustration or anxiety— your brain waves display disorganized, erratic patterns. A steady consistent heartbeat (heart rate coherence) is a sign of a brain ready to learn. *Heart Smart* is a focused breathing activity that helps steady your heartbeat to a balanced, consistent pattern (McCraty et al., 2001) in order to stabilize your brain waves so you can learn.

What to Do:

1. Focus your attention on your heart (put your hand over it to help you locate it in your mind).
2. Pretend you are breathing through your heart. Keep your focus there for ten seconds or longer.
3. Recall a memory of a fun or positive event and attempt to re-experience it. Don't just see it—try to feel, hear and live the memory with as many senses as possible. Turn it into a *feeling, physical* memory instead of just a mental one.
4. Take slow, deep breaths for thirty seconds.

Variation:

Try this breathing technique while performing any other *Energize* exercise.

Hook Up to Rewire Your Emotions

Purpose of this Activity:
When you feel a strong emotion, such as sadness, confusion, anxiety or anger, your body sends chemical messengers either to the amygdala and frontal cortex (to trigger a problem-solving response) or to the brain stem region (to trigger an automatic, "fight or flight" response). For some students, practicing a skill they find difficult or facing an

assignment they have no confidence they can finish induces the brain stem response. Very little cognition will happen until their emotional messaging system is calmed. When the emotional response is no longer in control of their thinking process, they are free to respond to new information using the rational thinking areas of the brain. These emotional response pathways are usually established at infancy by means of sucking motions and cross-lateral motor movements. *Hook Up to Rewire Your Emotions* helps calm the emotional response by activating the pathways in both hemispheres of the sensory-motor cortex that were established in infancy (Hannaford, 1995).

What to Do:
1. Stand up and cross your legs at the ankle. Keep them crossed.
2. Cross your straight arms at the wrist and lace your fingers together.
3. Bring your hands to your heart, turning them so your interlaced fingers are up and your crossed wrists are down.
4. Breathe deeply with your tongue pressed flat against the roof of your mouth.

5. Relax your tongue as you exhale through your nose.
6. Remain in this position and continue this breathing cycle for one minute.
7. Uncross your legs and arms.
8. Put your fingertips and palms together and rest your hands comfortably against your stomach.
9. Continue the breathing cycle, taking deep breaths, inhaling with your tongue pressed flat against the roof of your mouth and exhaling with your tongue relaxed.
10. Remain in this position and continue this breathing cycle for one to two minutes or until you feel calm.

Variation:
Perform this activity while sitting or lying down.

Lymphatic Flush

Purpose of this Activity:
The lymph nodes and the clear lymphatic fluid that flows from them into the bloodstream are one part of the body's waste removal system. Lymphatic fluid gathers dead cells, cellular waste and excess water and carries them to the bloodstream for elimination and processing. A strong flow of lymphatic fluid helps keep your neurons clean and ready to fire. In the 1930s, the osteopathic physician Frank Champman (who combined joint manipulation with eastern and western medical practices to treat ailments) discovered and mapped the nerve stimulation points that enhance lymphatic flow. These stimulation points are located primarily in the chest, in the spaces between the ribs next to the sternum and also along the spine (Promislow, 2000).

Lymphatic Flush exercises help mechanically stimulate lymphatic flow and indirectly help sharpen your ability to learn by keeping your neurons free from the interference of waste.

What to Do:
1. With one hand, massage the hollows on both sides of the breastbone, just below your collarbone.
2. Place your other hand on top of your navel.
3. Massage your collarbone points on both sides for one to two minutes.
4. Keep your hand on your navel area and, with your other hand, massage above and below the lips using your thumb and index finger. Massage your lip area for one to two minutes.
5. Keep your fingers on your lips and move the hand on your navel to your tailbone area.
6. Massage your lips and your tailbone for thirty seconds and then have your hands trade places.
7. Keep massaging your lips and your tailbone for twenty to thirty more seconds, all the while imagining your breath running up and down your spine.

Block Buster

Purpose of this Activity:
Negative memories or our perceptions of situations can cause us to feel or act edgy. Test anxiety, lack of recall and other stressors only add to a student's frustration and negatively impact his or her emotional state. The ability to access memory is dependent on emotional, physical and mental states. Recall becomes easier when you enter physical and emotional states similar to the ones you were in

while first learning the material (Bower & Morrow, 1990; Bower et al., 1992). Deep breathing while rubbing neurovascular points on the forehead will direct blood flow from the hypothalamus (part of the emotional processing system in the brain) to the frontal lobes, where rational thought occurs, as well as relax and calm the mind and body.

What to Do:
Perform a *Block Buster* whenever you need to access your memory to take a test or remember something like a speech, during homework sessions, or whenever you feel apprehensive, anxious, or frustrated.

1. Place your fingertips gently on your forehead above your eyebrows.
2. Push your skin very slightly toward your hairline. Imagine yourself trying to remember some bit of information for a test or performing a potentially stress-producing activity like giving a speech in public.
3. Imagine yourself remembering and succeeding on the test or being poised and confident while giving your speech.

Variation:
Perform *Block Busters* in conjunction with the breathing technique from *Heart Smart*: Imagine that you are breathing through your heart and think of only positive memories or events.

Sweep Away Stress

Purpose of this Activity:

Thinking is the process of accessing prior knowledge and either expanding it or creating new models of understanding it. These models are represented linguistically, symbolically

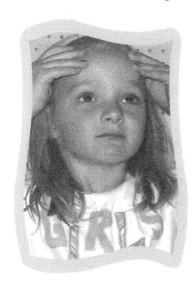

or with sensory memories that include smell, sound or tactile sensations (Pavio, 1969, 1971, 1990; Richardson, 1983). Practitioners of neuro-linguistic programming (NLP), a technique used by counselors and hypnotists to teach someone to function as if they were already an expert at the behavior they want to acquire, claim that certain eye movement patterns are indicative of specific sensory components represented in thought. For example, looking up and to the right indicates that you are imagining the way something would look if it were different than how you currently see it; other relationships between eye patterns and cognition are explained in NLP literature. Studies demonstrate that eye movements share a relationship with some aspects of cognitive functioning, although specific patterns have not yet been consistently observed (Jensen, 2000a; Dooley & Farmer, 1988). A full eye rotation, one that extends the eye muscles in all directions, activates all the sensory imaging areas of the brain at once (Topping, 1990).

What to Do:

This exercise may be performed with your eyes open or closed—you choose!

1. Place your fingertips between your eyebrows and your hairline on both sides of your forehead. Feel around until you find the tender spots (they should be above your pupils).
2. Gently push the skin of your forehead toward your hairline and hold it there.
3. Slowly rotate your eyes clockwise slightly beyond 360 degrees.
4. Then, slowly rotate your eyes counterclockwise slightly beyond 360 degrees.
5. Repeat this cycle of eye rotations, keeping your eye muscles fully extended until the eyes rotate smoothly in both directions.
6. As you perform this exercise, mentally recite a self-motivating mantra, such as, "I feel calm and ready to learn," or, "Ideas for writing come easily to me."

Chill Out

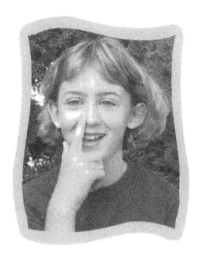

Purpose of this Activity:
Our normal breathing pattern is a polarized one; it regularly alternates between nostrils, balancing the ionization of potassium and calcium in the blood. Stress depolarizes the cell membranes of neurons, which reduces their electrical potential for excitation (the process neurons use to communicate with each other). Polarized cells have the means to respond quickly to stimuli; depolarized cells have a slower response rate (Hannaford, 1995). Breathing cycles shift from one nostril to the other throughout the day, helping to cool and oxygenate one hemisphere of the brain and then the other. These cycles are also linked to hemispheric dominance. Polarized breathing can help activate both sides of the brain for easier access to all regions of the brain (Shannahoff-Khalsa, 1983). This activity was first used by Dr. Sheldon Deal in 1973 and has been clinically demonstrated to help balance the brain and body for relaxation and better thinking.

What to Do:
1. Place your tongue against the roof of your mouth.
2. Lightly press the right nostril shut and inhale through the left nostril.
3. Press the left nostril shut and release the right nostril to exhale.
4. Repeat this cycle three times.
5. Switch nostrils so that you press the left nostril shut to inhale through the right nostril and press the right nostril shut to exhale through the left nostril.
6. Repeat this cycle three times.

4 Activate Large Muscles for Optimal Learning

What the Research Says...

About Balancing...

Balance is an adaptive, complex behavior dependent on our ability to overcome imbalance. The cerebellum receives information from the inner ear (vestibular system) and alerts the eyes (visual system) and the pressure sensors of the joints, muscles, and skin (proprioceptive system) that the gravitational relationship of the body to the environment has changed and that some postural action is needed (or else you'll fall down!). This signal activates the sensors in the muscles and connective tissues of the proprioceptive system, which send information to the brain about the location of the muscles and joints in space. Meanwhile, the eyes process visual cues and provide other information the brain needs to monitor the body's position. In this way, your body is able accommodate gravity and its effects on you in your present position.

To maintain balance, two of those three systems must work well (Haybach, 2001). Students with an immature control of their balance often lose their concentration and begin wiggling within fifteen to twenty minutes of a sitting session. For these students, movement gathers the information the brain needs to maintain the body's posture but that the senses do not provide (Gold, 2002).

About the Vestibular System...

The vestibular system is commonly known as the balancing system, the inner ear system or the equilibrium sense. In the ear are three fluid-filled, semicircular canals (superior, posterior and lateral), set at right angles to each other, and two vestibular sacs (utricle and saccule), also filled with fluid. Any movement of the body (especially movement of the head) sets the fluid in motion. Hair cells, sensitive to movement, line the insides of the sacs and canals and transmit to the brain information about the body's changing relationship to space. The cerebellum, which is receiving information from the eyes and muscle cells simultaneously, interprets the vestibular signals from the inner ear and directs the visual and proprioceptive systems to alter the body's posture as necessary. Interestingly, the vestibular system can play a large role in a student's school performance. A pediatric physician tracked a group of normal infants and vestibularly disabled infants for three years and found that children with vestibular problems also demonstrated delays in motor development, balance, language acquisition, reading and writing (De Quiros, 1976).

Because vestibular receptors are located in the eyes, muscles and joints as well as in the inner ear, the vestibular processing system is unique. The vestibular system coordinates information from the inner ear *and* other parts of the body.

Dr. Steven Cool of Pacific University in Forest Grove, Oregon compared the five commonly known senses (smell, sight, hearing, feeling, and tasting) to the vestibular system and found that unlike the other senses, the vestibular systems not only has ascending nerve pathways to the brain, but also descending pathways to other sensory monitoring areas. For example, your sense of smell is limited to one-way communication with the brain, which means that the odor receptors in your nose can only send sensory input to the brain; they never receive information from it. Your brain can interpret signals as the scent of a flower but it cannot direct your nose to behave in any way other than as a passive collector of environmental smells. It can, however, consider the movement of your body and signal a muscle to relax or tense in order to keep you balanced as you climb a steep hill or float on a raft in a swimming pool.

The Organs of the Ear

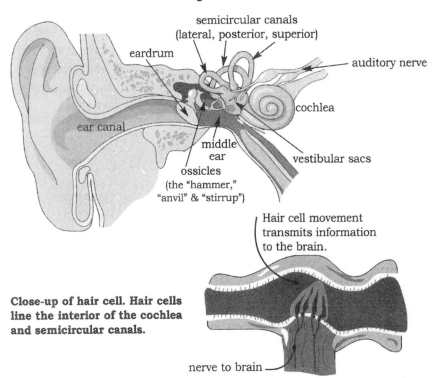

semicircular canals
(lateral, posterior, superior)

eardrum

auditory nerve

ear canal

cochlea

middle ear

vestibular sacs

ossicles
(the "hammer,"
"anvil" & "stirrup")

Hair cell movement transmits information to the brain.

Close-up of hair cell. Hair cells line the interior of the cochlea and semicircular canals.

nerve to brain

About Hemispherical Communication...

Our brain is divided into two hemispheres, each with interrelated, specialized functions. A band of myelinated networks, the corpus callosum, keeps the two hemispheres in constant communication with each other. Cross-lateral motor movements, which move a limb from one side of the body across the midline to perform a task on the other side, develop the corpus callosum more fully than do regular movements (Hannaford, 1995). When scientists looked at Albert Einstein's brain after his death, the most significant difference between his and the brain of a common man was that Einstein's corpus callosum was highly myelinated and much thicker (Diamond & Hopson, 1999). Now, developing a thicker corpus callosum will probably not make you as brilliant as Einstein, but it is nonetheless reasonable to state that the repeated performance of activities known to increase the myelination of the neurons connecting both hemispheres of the brain will benefit anyone.

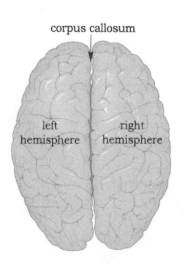

corpus callosum

left hemisphere   right hemisphere

What the Research Means

When students enter your class with an underdeveloped sense of touch, body position or movement and gravity, simple tasks like sitting in a chair while holding a book and moving their eyes left to right across a page may be so overwhelming that their brains focus only on basic safety and survival needs and pay no attention to new learning (Gabbard, 1998). Instead of understanding the information presented in your lesson, they are distracted by their brains' instinctive effort to keep them out of danger.

So who are the students in class you need to *activate* for focused learning? Singh Sideliner, who doesn't participate in games, swinging or sliding activities during recess and who is prone to motion sickness as well. Dizzy Darius, who swings or spins constantly. Clumsy Cleo, who awkwardly walks through the classroom, accidentally bumping into desks and chairs. These three students could benefit from exercises that improve their balance and movement systems. Just the thought of moving makes Singh nervous; Darius does whatever he can to wake up his vestibular sense; Cleo has no idea why she is so clumsy despite her carefulness.

The degree to which these behaviors interfere with learning varies from case to case. Children with severely dysfunctional vestibular systems require attention from specialists.

Symptoms of vestibular dysfunction include:
- fear of moving through space—swinging, teeter-tottering, going down a slide
- poor balance in motor activities; avoidance of activities that challenge balance
- seeking excessive movement on the play ground—jumping, spinning or swinging—when compared to peers of the same age
- hesitation to climb or descend stairs
- frequent falls
- motion sickness
- continuous motion; for example, an inability to sit still for an activity and a constant display of activity in the form of rocking back and forth or frequently changing position in order to sit on the feet, leg or knee

The proprioceptive system provides information to the brain about the body's position in relationship to space. Body awareness is necessary to motor control and planning. It is what allows us to walk smoothly, climb stairs, sit, lie down or even learn to write! When we monitor the pressure with which we push on a pencil, the strength of our grip and the relationship of our hand to the paper, we are relying upon proprioceptive feedback (Cheatum & Hammond, 2000). Students who do not have a well-developed sense of their body are easy to identify.

Wanda Wall-Clinger, who leans her back against the wall and side-steps down the hallway in order to stimulate the proprioceptors in her muscles and joints and orient herself in space. Randy Ricochet, who bounces in the doorway whenever he exits or enters a room, who can see an obstacle in his path but lacks the body awareness to avoid hitting it. These students twist and chew on their clothing and watch their feet while going up and down stairs. They are often dismissed as merely uncoordinated.

Symptoms of proprioceptive dysfunction include:
- tendency to fatigue more easily than peers
- apparent lack of physical strength
- inability to jump, hop, skip or run as well as other children of the same age
- awkward or stiff movements
- bumping into people and things
- inability to locate the body in space
- confusion with identifying left and right
- hesitation to play on climbing apparatus
- preference for table activities instead of field games

- difficulty mastering new motor tasks
- difficulty playing rhythmic clapping games
- inability to pump self on a swing

Transitioning to Activate Exercises

Hint: Explaining the reason for performing these exercises is just as important as telling students how to do them. For example, try this introduction:

"Today we want as many parts of our brain working together as possible. First, we'll activate our large muscles and then our small ones."

Hint: Plan carefully. Select only the activities that can be performed freely and comfortably within the space available.

Hint: Let your class enjoy some of the benefits of physical exercise. Some activities involving large muscles can be aerobic if they are performed for at least five minutes, which is long enough to elevate the heart rate, supply the body with large amounts of oxygen and trigger feel-good endorphins.

Hint: Physical activity is good for the body but can dehydrate it as well. Make sure students have ready access to water and plenty of opportunity to drink it.

Activities

Whirling and Twirling

Materials Needed:
Unobstructed space for each
person to stand with their
arms extended from their
shoulders and spin

Purpose of this Activity:
Studies of astronaut
training programs indicate that daily exposure to bodily
spinning and rotation over the course of two weeks signifi-
cantly improves normal walking and the performance of other
motor skills (Secades, 1984; Dobie et al., 1990; Griffin &
Brett, 1997; Reschke et al., 1998; Prothero et al.,
1999). Hyperactive children who spin for thirty seconds in
either direction show an increase in attention span for up to
thirty minutes afterwards (Goddard, 2002). Furthermore, students who participate in spinning routines show significant
gains in measures of attention and reading (Palmer, 1980).

What to Do:
1. Stand and extend your hands straight out to the sides
   with your palms down.
2. Spin as fast as is comfortable for fifteen seconds in
   either direction.
3. Stop and close your eyes, keeping your balance
   while standing still for fifteen seconds.
4. Repeat, for two to five minutes, the sequence of spinning
   for fifteen seconds and resting for fifteen seconds.

Note:

Keep the following suggestions in mind to reap the best results from *Whirling and Twirling.*

1. Instruct students to keep their heads up.
2. Provide clear and easy-to-see visual cues to focus on during the spinning to reduce dizziness.
3. Speed matters. Urge your students to spin as fast as they can without making themselves sick or falling down.
4. Alternate the direction of the spinning throughout the exercise session (Cool, 2003).

Cross Overs

Purpose of this Activity:

Cross Overs stimulate the right hemisphere and left hemisphere of the brain in an alternating fashion, building up nerve networks across the corpus callosum (Kranowitz, 2003). Slowly performing this cross-lateral activity forces the fine motor muscles in the eyes, ears and joints to maintain balance for longer periods of time. The more you can stimulate and activate these nerve pathways, the more myelinated they will become and the more quickly they will respond to stimuli (Tortora & Anagnostakos, 1990). This exercise activates several different areas in our brain at the same time: the right and left hemispheres of the brain (related to cognitive skills, attention and the sensory motor system), the basal ganglia in the limbic system (related to the systems of pleasure and reward), and the cerebellum (related to memory and the sensory motor system) (Hannaford, 1995). It enhances learning because it engages and warms up many different parts of the brain.

What to Do:

1. Very deliberately and slowly, touch your arms to the opposite legs. (For example, touch your left knee with your right hand or elbow and then touch your right knee with your left hand or elbow.) Repeat this movement ten times.
2. Then, touch your arms to the legs on the same side. Repeat this movement five times on each side.
3. Alternate between cross-body and one-side movements three or four times.
4. Finish by doing a final series of cross-body movements.

Variations:

1. Perform these movements while sitting, standing or lying on your back.
2. Perform these movements in front of your body or behind your back.
3. Perform these movements with your eyes closed to help improve balance.
4. Skip or bounce between touches.

Lateral Tapping

Materials Needed:
A chair for each child; metronome (optional)

Purpose of this Activity:
Lateral Tapping is a cross-body exercise that increases the number of myelinated nerves between the brain's right and left hemispheres and develops a learner's ability to identify the left and right sides of the body. Students will find it easier to follow directions in reading, writing and math if they have an internalized sense of left and right (Blaydes-Madigan, 2001). The activity's stomping and hitting motions stimulate the proprioceptive receptors that

feed the brain information about which muscles have been activated on what side of the body; calling out the name and location of a body part (left foot, right hand) stimulates the language receptors; movements on one side of the body become associated with the words "left" and "right" (Richards & Remick, 1988). Sometimes it is not possible or practical to move around the room in order to activate the three movement-related systems. *Lateral Tapping* allows students to engage these systems without having to leave their seats.

What to Do:
For two or three minutes, tap out various rhythms against your body and have your student repeat the pattern.
1. Sit in a chair, with both of your feet on the ground and one hand on each knee to start.
2. Determine a pattern that your students will have to repeat. Begin with three-step patterns and advance as students become more skilled. One sequence might be to tap your left thigh with your left hand, tap your right thigh with your right hand and then stomp both of your feet. Model the pattern and then have them copy it a minimum of three times.
3. Encourage the students to orally repeat the pattern as they are performing it.
4. Increase the difficulty of the pattern by increasing the number of steps in the pattern. You may use the same pattern the entire time, or stop and demonstrate a more complex pattern to do. It's up to you.

Variations:
1. Verbally state the pattern to be followed but do not model it. You can write the steps out for students to read if they cannot keep the pattern in their memory.
2. Require that students perform the repeating pattern to a steady beat.
3. Vary the tempo of the pattern.
4. Have a student volunteer lead the class by tapping out rhythms for everyone else (including you!) to follow.

Don't Rock the Boat!

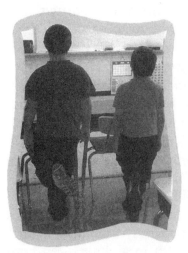

Purpose of this Activity:

The most advanced level of balance is the ability to stay still. Any type of movement, including sitting, involves maintaining equilibrium in relationship to gravity. Students with the wiggles often do not feel the pull of gravity and move just to stimulate the vestibular system for the additional feedback they need (Riehle et al., 1997). The action of *not* moving requires whole body functions and muscle groups to operate together with continuous, imperceptible adjustments, and signifies the advent of mature postural control (Goddard, 2002). Practicing balancing activities stimulates the equilibrium cycle and prepares the body to sit still.

What to Do:

1. Stand with your feet slightly spread apart.
2. Raise one foot about ten inches off the floor and hold the balance for a minimum of five seconds. Switch feet.
3. Next, balance on one foot and swing your other leg back and forth ten times. Switch.
4. To understand the role vision plays during balancing, repeat any one of the balances with your eyes closed.

Variations:

1. Increase the level of a balance's difficulty by closing your eyes and rotating them under your eyelids.
2. Write your name in the air with one foot while balancing on the other.
3. Practice math facts or spelling words by writing numbers or letters in the air with one foot while balancing on the other.

Wake Up the Little Brain

Purpose of this Activity:
When you notice that your students are restless or fatigued, wake them up! These exercises stimulate the neurons in the cerebellum (Latin for "little brain"), which was long thought to control movement. There is mounting evidence, however, that this part of the brain is involved in many other functions, too, most notably sensory functions like working memory, attention, impulse control and spatial planning (Bower & Parsons, 2003). Movement and learning are inexorably linked (Mushiake & Strick, 1995), and both require oxygen as fuel. But because the brain cannot store oxygen like the other organs in the body, it constantly needs a fresh supply (Greenfield, 1996). Large muscle work rapidly circulates oxygenated blood through the body to give your brain the energy it needs to function.

What to Do:
Select one or more of the exercises below and stay in motion for two to five minutes.

1. While sitting in a chair, vigorously stomp your feet on the floor ten times, or, rock and shift your weight from side to side ten times.
2. Scoot your chair back so there are twelve inches between your stomach and your desk. Place your hands flat on the desk, shoulder-width apart, as if you were about to do push-ups. Then, do ten seated push-ups (keep your bottom in the chair). Make your push-ups nice and slow, and expend as much muscular effort as possible.
3. Do five chair lift-ups by placing your hands next to your thighs on the seat of your chair and pushing down to lift your bottom off the chair.

Crazy Eights

Materials Needed:
Large, open area with room to walk in a figure eight pattern without having to worry about running into others

Purpose of this Activity:
The right side of the brain controls the left side of the body and the left side of the brain controls the right side of the body. The more myelinated nerve fibers you have between your brain's hemispheres, the more easily you can switch between hemispheric processing centers and use both sides of the brain. Even walking a straight line requires the right

and left hemisphere to shift from supporting and balancing the body's weight to moving a leg forward. Walking with opposing arms opens another nerve pathway between the hemispheres. All of us mastered the alternating leg movement when we learned to walk but not everyone has mastered the next step: swinging the arms. You can develop this skill by walking in any pattern—straight line, circle or triangle—but walking in a figure eight with deliberate, opposing arm and leg movements allows you to also alternately turn to the left and then the right. This extra element presents another opportunity to develop the nerve pathways between the right and left hemispheres of your brain.

What to Do:

When you first introduce this activity to your class, begin by leading your students as a group through a very large figure eight pattern. Have the students follow you through the pattern until they are familiar with its turns and can walk smaller figure eights without your direction. Walk figure eight patterns often. Each time you perform this activity, practice one of these suggested improvements:

Improve Opposing Arm Movements for Walking:
1. Swing your arms evenly and continuously throughout the entire walk. Make sure that your right arm swings forward when your left foot takes a step and that your left arm swings forward when your right foot takes a step.
2. Swing your arms an equal distance forward and back.
3. Swing your arms from the shoulders, not the elbows. Stay relaxed and flexible.
4. Keep your hands open and relaxed.

Improve Breathing:
1. Maintain a continuous, deep, relaxed breathing pattern.
2. Keep your back relaxed so the rib cage can expand completely.

Improve Foot and Leg Movements:
1. Place each foot heel to toe, making sure all five of your toes gently touch the floor before you take your next step.
2. Make sure both feet point in the same direction that you are walking.
3. Relax your knees to cushion the impact of each foot as it makes contact with the floor.

Improve Head Placement:
Keep your neck, forehead, eyes, jaw, throat and tongue relaxed.

Variation:

Advance other skills by mentally rehearsing them as you walk in *Crazy Eights*.

1. Practice seeing patterns and extending them in your mind's eye (1a, 2b, 3c, 4d, ...).
2. Think of numbers and their Roman numeral representations; count from zero to one hundred by threes, fours, sixes, sevens or eights.
3. Strengthen finger movement control by touching your thumb to each finger on the same hand.
4. Prioritize your goals for the day, week or month.
5. Mentally compose power statements that affirm your abilities and talents.

5 Lead "Sense"-ibly

What the Research Says...

About Auditory Processing...

Hearing and auditory processing are not the same. If someone with perfect hearing has difficulties with auditory processing, the brain may not be able to interpret the heard sounds correctly. Efficient auditory processing depends on a good sense of hearing *and* auditory discrimination skills, the body's ability to rapidly transmit auditory information to the appropriate area in the brain and to screen out irrelevant sounds (Goddard, 2002). Temporary auditory processing deficits can be an underlying cause of a student's inability to read, by contributing to a lack of proficiency in identifying the sounds of a word (phonemic awareness), a lack of proficiency in associating sounds with printed symbols (phonics), and the inability to hold information in the auditory memory long enough to remember the sequence of the letters in a word or words in a sentence

(Fawcett et al., 1996). These deficits can be improved or eliminated with activities designed to improve auditory processing skills (Temple et al., 2000).

About the Visual System...

Visual processing is the brain's ability to interpret information taken in through the eyes. This is different from being able to see clearly at a given distance. Problems understanding spatial relationships, the inability to use visual discrimination or visual closure skills to consistently recognize objects and poor visual motor skills are all common aspects of difficulty with visual processing. The muscular subskills of visual processing required for schoolwork include the ability to track objects, shift focus, hold items in focus and use both eyes equally. A study published in the prestigious *Journal of Behavioral Optometry* found that more than eighty-five percent of participating students with both behavior and academic problems failed a visual test. The documented difficulties most noted were with tracking, near and far visual acuity, and binocular depth perception (Johnson et al., 1996). This finding supports earlier research that determined a significant correlation between binocular focusing abilities and academic performance (Metzer & Schur, 1967).

About Fine Motor Functioning...

The neuromotor system has three components to it: *gross motor function*, which involves the large muscles used in sitting, standing, and moving; *fine motor function* (specifically manual dexterity), which is used to create and build objects, play a musical instrument and type on a keyboard; and *graphomotor function*, which is directly related to using a utensil to produce handwriting (Levine, 2003). When you use your fingers to construct and create, your fine motor subskills, like grasping or hand-eye coordination, work together to complete the project. To write and form letters, many muscles and nerve receptors must cooperate. Extensive research has demonstrated that the development of accurate speed and legible handwriting is a long process—one that often breaks down (Smits-Engelsman & Van Galen, 1997; Van Galen et al., 1991), possibly affecting writing and composition skills. If the brain is busy remembering how to form a letter and where to put words on a paper (or where to place the finger on the keyboard to make it type the letter needed for the word), then the mental space available for thoughts and ideas is limited (Smits-Engelsman & Van Galen, 1997). Because the key to expressing thoughts in writing is to have the production skill of writing *or* typing at an automatic level, it is fortunate that someone with poor graphomotor skills can still learn to type and poor typists can improve their handwriting skills. Computer technology holds promise for those who cannot master the graphomotor skills, as long as they are given opportunities to learn to type by touch.

What the Research Means

We generally name the five senses as sight, hearing, touch, taste and smell. Actually, we have seven sensory processing loops that continuously feed the brain with information and enable our body to respond to the brain's subsequent directions: the sensory input from our inner ear and muscles form the *vestibular* and *proprioceptive* processing loops that sense body movements and send out corrective messages to the muscles and joints to keep us in balance (1 & 2); the eyes run visual input through the *visual processing* loop (3); the ears send signals through the *auditory processing* system (4); the skin collects the tactile data needed to manipulate the *fine motor processing* system (5); the nose and tongue work together to process information about *taste* (6); and the nose enables the sense of *smell* (7). The senses used most often in school settings are sight, hearing, touch, the vestibular system and the proprioceptive system. Occupational therapists Billye Ann Cheatum and Allison Hammond, authors of *Physical Activities for Improving*

Children's Learning and Behavior (Human Kinetics: 2000), present the following as an overview of the sensory systems most needed for school work:

Sense*	Sensory Organs	Sensory System	School Skill
Balance	ears	vestibular	sitting, standing, maintaining a posture
Movement	joints and muscles	proprioceptive	maintaining a posture, moving safely through space and around obstacles
Touch	skin	tactile	fine motor activities
Sight	eyes	visual	reading/writing
Hearing	ears	auditory	communicating/ understanding

*Taste and smell are not included in this list because their sensory input is rarely used to learn within the classroom setting.

Studies have found that developing skills to the point where they can be performed automatically frees the cerebral space and mental energy to perform more complex tasks such as problem-solving, or composing and writing thoughts in a coherent manner (Jones & Christensen, 1999; Mon-Williams et al., 1999). One way to improve academic abilities, therefore, is to improve the visual, auditory and fine motor skills used for learning. The previous chapter, *Activate Large Muscles for Optimal Learning*, listed and explained the activities that enhance students' proprioceptive and vestibular processing systems; the exercise sets in this chapter deal specifically with the visual system, the auditory system and fine motor movement system in the hands. For years, occupational therapists have been using the exercises in this chapter to develop the automaticity of the skills needed for processing auditory, visual or tactile input efficiently. You can use them, too.

Listening and Communication: Activate the Auditory System

Whenever we ask students to sit and listen, we assume that they have the skills to process what they hear and apply it. Many times, however, students do not have the ability to hold information in their mind long enough to process all of it. They would benefit from practice with auditory processing skills.

So who are the students that may have a dysfunction of the auditory system? Riesa Repeat-It-For-Me, who can follow the first of three given directions but has to ask someone what to do next. Miguel Misspeller, who still doesn't grasp the letter-sound relationship even after repeated interventions. Donna Distractible, who doesn't seem to listen when you are talking, but instead looks around or away from you as you speak. The activities in this section are designed to help with the development of the auditory system.

Symptoms of auditory processing dysfunction include:

- hypersensitivity to loud sounds, like bells or the flush of a toilet
- difficulty speaking clearly enough for others to understand
- apparent difficulty understanding or paying attention to what is said
- high awareness of and easily distracted by sounds that others do not notice, like the humming of fluorescent lights
- difficulty executing two- or three-step directions

Transitioning to these Exercises

Hint: Explaining the reason for performing these exercises is just as important as telling students how to do them. For example, try this introduction:

"We should warm up our sensory systems before we do our (math, science, reading, writing etc.) lesson. Because we'll need to use our (eyes, ears, hands) today, we'll warm them up by doing (name the activity)."

Hint: A *Lead* exercise is last exercise you perform before the actual lesson begins. To kick off the lesson in a brain-friendly way, review prior knowledge or introduce new information while you are performing the exercise.

Hint: Different parts of a lesson require different auditory, visual or fine motor skills. When you shift from one part of the lesson to the next, perform a different *Lead* activity to support the sensory skill needed for the next portion of the lesson.

Activities

Ear Lobe Roll

Purpose of this Activity:
The ear contains more than four hundred acupressure points related to almost all of the functions of the brain and body; the *Ear Lobe Roll* exercise stimulates more than 148

of them. Massaging these pressure points excites the reticular activating system of the brain, which tunes out distracting noises and sounds while awakening the whole hearing mechanism (Deal, 1973; Hannaford, 1995). Students spend a great deal of their day listening to teachers and peers to gain new knowledge. As the hearing system begins to fatigue, their ability to screen out background noise and focus on the important noise (lecture or classroom discussions) diminishes. By activating the reticular activating system and the sensory systems associated with hearing, *Ear Lobe Roll* helps the body's noise filter function more effectively.

What to Do:

1. At the top of your ear next to your scalp, use your thumb and forefinger to gently pull up on your ear and unroll the cartilage.
2. Continue to pull and gently unroll your ear as you move down the side of the ear to the fleshy lobe.
3. For one to two minutes, massage both ears simultaneously as you repeat the process from top to bottom and then the bottom to top, repeatedly.

Repeat After Me

Purpose of this Activity:

The ability to distinguish slight variances in sound and rhythms and then remember what you heard is known as auditory discrimination and sequential memory (Cheatum & Hammond, 2000). This skill is critical to learning to read and spell because it is the foundation to the emergence of phonemic awareness, or the ability to discriminate and identify the sounds in a word. Phonemic awareness is similar to phonics, but is considered a pre-skill for developing the sound-symbol relationship (Torgesen et al., 2003). *Repeat After Me* will enhance phonemic awareness by training the auditory system to hear and process sounds with a variety of characteristics.

What to Do:

1. Instruct your students to listen carefully because they will have to repeat what you do.
2. On your desk, tap out a pattern four to seven sounds long, depending on the ability of your students. Vary the sounds by tapping softly, loudly, slowly or rapidly.

3. Repeat the pattern two times. (Students will hear the pattern three times in all.)
4. Have your students repeat the tapping pattern *exactly* as they heard it, duplicating not only the number of taps but also the elements of volume, rhythm and timing.

Memory Stretcher

Purpose of this Activity:
Auditory memory is the ability to hear language, hold it in memory and act on the information (Schneider, 2001). When you ask students to get out a pencil, a piece of paper, scissors and their math book, you are exercising their auditory memory. Reading and comprehension rely on a form of auditory memory as well. Whether articulated aloud or read silently, words take on a *voice*; the reader has to remember that voice and its message in the first part of a sentence while reading the end of that sentence in order to comprehend its meaning (Furr, 2000). This exercise develops auditory memory by explicitly practicing this skill.

What to Do:
1. Announce that you are going to give some instructions for students to listen to carefully and then follow. Start with just three steps and increase the length of the list as student skill increases.
2. Model the process so students know what to do and then give the instructions.
3. When students have finished following the instructions, ask them to tell a neighbor what they did and in what order.

Sample Instructions:
1. "Stand up, push in your chair and turn around once."
2. "Lift your left foot, lift your right foot and put your head down."
3. "Take out a piece of paper, put your name on it and raise your hand."

Dot-Dot-Dash

Materials Needed:
Paper and pencil

Purpose of this Activity:
Letters and numerals are symbolic representations that we use to interpret what we read and to understand mathematical concepts. Each symbol is linked to at least one associated auditory sound. It is one thing to hear the word "three" and know what it means and still another to see the symbol "3" and know that it represents "three" (Mahony et al., 2000). The process of matching auditory information to visual symbols is a foundational skill for reading, writing and mathematics. Taking notes during class and taking a spelling test are just two of the common activities that require a student to have the ability to match a *word* with a symbol or series of symbols (Burgess & Lonigon, 1998). *Dot-Dot-Dash* helps students improve their ability to match auditory and visual information with a simplified code. The use of dots and dashes instead of letters to record sounds enables this exercise to focus on listening for two different sounds and recording two different symbols without invoking the very complex connotations and meanings of the alphanumerical code that may cognitively distract your students.

What to Do:

1. Blow a whistle, tap a pencil against the desk or use any convenient sound maker to create a pattern of intermittent long and short sounds similar to Morse code.
2. On paper, have students transcribe the pattern by using a dot to represent a short sound and a dash to represent a long sound. If necessary, repeat the pattern for students who may need extra practice with this skill.
3. Start with very simple combinations and gradually increase their complexity. (You may find it helpful to write your patterns on a card before performing them for your students; it can sometimes be difficult to remember the longer combinations and you need to be able to reproduce them exactly.)

Sample Patterns:

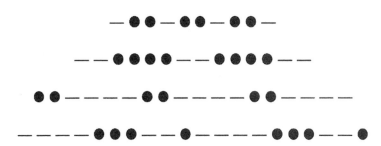

Reading and Writing:
Activate the Visual System

Reading and writing are subject areas that depend heavily on the visual processing system. Students who have trouble with reading or writing may have underdeveloped visual processing skills even if they have perfect vision. If they display poor hand-eye or foot-eye coordination, they may lack the visual skills to track moving objects. If they have poor reading comprehension skills, they may not have well-developed visualization abilities.

Visualization is the non-linguistic representation of thoughts or ideas. The *dual coding* theory of information storage (memory) postulates that knowledge is stored in two forms: a linguistic form and imagery form (Richardson, 1983). Whether or not teachers realize it, they commonly engage students in creating non-linguistic representations every time they assign the task of drawing a diagram during a science lesson or record a brainstorming session with a colorful idea map. The more often we employ both systems of representation, the better we are able to think and recall knowledge (Marzano et al., 2001). Electroencephalograms (EEGs) of brainwave activity taken when students are engaged in creating non-linguistic representations show an increased activity in the brain (Gerlic & Jausovec, 1999).

An Oxford University study found that visualization before an exercise improves learning. One group of elementary students was led through a practice visualization and make-believe session before taking a test; the control group was not. The group that pre-visualized scored better on the test than the other group (Drake, 1996). This supports the notion that students can improve reading comprehension, writing fluency and creativity, and problem-solving skills by developing strong visualizing skills. But which students demonstrate visual processing dysfunctions?

Wyatt Whiffer, who can never seem to hit the ball that is pitched during in softball games. Missy Missed-It, who can't see the ball to catch when she's in the field. Inez I-Don't-Get-It, who needs to have everything explained and shown to her and who most likely lacks the ability to translate language into visual images. Louis Lost-My-Place, who has trouble with reading exercises or activities that require him to copy material from the board. Extreme forms of visual system dysfunction should be referred to a vision therapist. For those students in your class with only mild or moderate problems with visual processing, the activities in this section may help them.

Symptoms of visual dysfunction include:
- difficulty naming or matching colors, shapes and sizes
- using trial and error techniques to complete puzzles
- reversing words, numbers and letters beyond the first grade
- difficulty following a moving object with the eyes
- trouble copying from the blackboard
- losing your place during reading exercises
- poor reading comprehension and trouble following directions

Transitioning to these Exercises

This activity section includes some exercises designed to improve visualization skills and others that strengthen the physical skills required for accurate eye muscle control. Visualization skill practice tends to take three to five minutes; physical eye exercises take less time. Choose whichever activity is most appropriate for your lesson.

Hint: Explaining the reason for performing these exercises is just as important as telling students how to do them. For example, try this introduction:

"In order to really understand something, make a picture of it in your mind. I am going to ask you to close your eyes and listen to what I describe. Attempt to really *see* whatever it is I am portraying."

Activities

Visualizations to Improve Reading Comprehension

Purpose of this Activity:
Visualization skills are essential to reading comprehension. The most efficient way to remember written material is to remember its concepts and ideas; concepts and ideas are best remembered as visual images (Marzano et al., 2001).

Perform this exercise each day to give your students practice generating visual images. After a few days of practice, only one sentence will be necessary for them to evoke lots of mental imagery. This exercise is an effective way to review the previous day's reading from content areas or from a piece of literature.

What to Do:

1. Orally give students descriptive words and phrases and ask them to visualize them. Try statements like, "The furry cat lounged lazily in the sun," "The moon was so bright it was difficult to see the stars in the sky," "The soccer player moved the ball so quickly down the field that the goalie didn't have time to prepare," and "If you don't hurry, you'll miss the bus!"
2. Between statements, ask students to indicate whether or not they were able to generate a visual image.

3. If your group seems uneasy about the process or some students report that they see only black, perform steps 4 and 5.
4. Relax, breathe deeply and close your eyes. Don't think of any words—just watch the black behind your eyelids.
5. After watching the black for about a minute, you will notice flashes of light or gradual spots of light appear. Keep watching, without thinking of anything in particular and then write down a brief description of what happened.
6. Perform this visualization exercise every day, afterwards always writing down a brief description of what happened.

Visualizations to Improve Writing

Purpose of this Activity:

Visualization can help you understand another person's point of view. Both imagining events to be unlike they were and creating images of different possibilities for the same initial event add flexibility to thinking. Being able to see from other viewpoints assists students when they must write a piece of work that involves conflicts and resolutions and when they must write for a specific audience.

What to Do:

1. Try to visualize how your day would have been if you had done the opposite of an action you performed. (What would have happened if you hadn't gotten out of bed? What if you had said yes to a request to borrow money instead of no? What if you had worn a sweater instead of a tee shirt?)
2. Visualize the events of your day in reverse. Identify anything you wish you had done differently.

3. If your students have trouble visualizing their activities in reverse, lead them through steps 4, 5 and 6.
4. Visualize a person you know well and respect. Picture this person doing an admirable deed. Next, imagine how you could imitate this person's admirable deed or respected quality to improve your effectiveness in relating to others.
5. Visualize a person behaving in a negative way. Now, erase that image and visualize the opposite; visualize that person performing the same activity but in a positive way.
6. Visualize a person that you have trouble relating to or like very little. Find one thing about that person you can admire and respect. Use this insight to help you understand that person better.

Note:

A lack of automaticity in handwriting is a significant factor in a child's ability to generate written text (Jones & Christensen, 1999). A simple way to improve a student's creative writing skill is to increase the automaticity of their handwriting or ability to use a computer keyboard. You may want to follow this visualization exercise with a fine motor activity from the next section of this chapter, *Tracking, Copying and Muscle Control: Activate the Fine Motor System.*

Creative Visualizations for Solving Problems

Purpose of this Activity:

Visual memory is only one aspect of the skill of visualization. It is not another term for visualization. Remembering a scene from your past in vivid pictorial detail is a type of visual memory. Being able to create an image out of nothing is creative visualization, sometimes known as mental elaboration. Studies suggest that this type of visualization is a powerful tool for enhancing recall and problem-solving ability (Antonietti et al., 1994; Antonietti, 1999; Willoughby et al., 1997). Students with creative problem-solving skills are more resourceful when they encounter a potentially frustrating task.

What to Do:
1. Sit, relax and breathe deeply several times.
2. Close your eyes and visualize a circle, square or triangle —whichever is easiest. Visualize the actual shape, not its representation as a word spelled with letters.
3. Change the form's size, add some color, change the color, decorate it with stripes and polka dots or alter its form in other ways. This may be difficult to do.
4. Practice making these changes. When you become skilled, try a shape with more sides or angles.

Tracking, Copying and Muscle Control: Activate the Fine Motor System

Tracking a line of print across a page or locating your place in a paragraph requires your eye muscles to work optimally (have you ever tried to read when you are sleepy?). These following exercises are designed to strengthen the muscles responsible for controlling these movements.

Transitioning to these Exercises

Hint: Explaining the reason for performing these exercises is just as important as telling students how to do them. For example, try this introduction:

"The muscles that control our eyes are very small but still need to be exercised. Let's take some time to strengthen them as a way to get ready for our reading lesson."

Hint: The visual system relies on as many as fifteen fine ocular motor skills. It is not unreasonable to lead visual warm-up sessions several times each day in order to boost the visual system. Perform at least two or three visual exercises in one day; this is a situation in which more is definitely better!

Hint: As they perform these exercises, students may complain about discomfort in their eyes, which may water or simply hurt. Be considerate. Allow students to relax their eyes by gazing at a distant object until the discomfort subsides; then, resume the exercise or begin the lesson, whichever is appropriate.

Activities

Head Turners

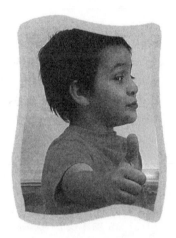

Purpose of this Activity:
Tracking is the ability to pursue materials with the eyes (ocular motor pursuit) in a smooth, fluid motion, whether they are objects and people traveling through space or lines of text in a book. To maintain attention during the task of reading, your eye must make several binocular fixations. In other words, both eyes must generate clear images that you hold and release as you encounter words or letters (Spache et al., 1992). First-graders who read one hundred words make about 230 fixations; adults make ninety or so fixations in a hundred word passage (Vogel, 1995). *Head Turners* strengthens the six muscles outside of each eye that are used to keep both eyes fixated on an object while the head is moving. Visual tracking ability improves when these muscles are exercised.

What to Do:
1. Stand in a relaxed posture with your weight equally distributed over both feet and your knees slightly bent.
2. Look at a target object at eye level, at least five feet away.
3. Keep both eyes on the target as you rotate your head from side to side, up and down, in a circle and diagonally for one to two minutes.

Thumbs Up

Purpose of this Activity:
Saccadic eye movements
are the precise locating
movements used for
jumping from one word to
another along a line of
print. These movements
involve the eyes only—the
head must remain sta-

tionary. Smooth saccadic movements are critical to
maintaining your place on the printed page (Richards &
Remick, 1988). Clinicians found that, among a group of one
hundred elementary-school children referred to a center for
reading disabilities to be screened for vision challenges,
forty-one percent of the children had visual tracking problems (Koslowe, 1995). Smooth tracking is required to
develop reading fluency, a skill closely correlated with reading comprehension (Torgesen et al., 2003). *Thumbs Up*
assists in the development of smooth, accurate eye movements and increases the ability to see peripherally—
important skills for developing literacy.

What to Do:
1. Stand in a relaxed posture with your weight equally
   distributed over both feet and your knees slightly bent.
2. Extend your right arm in front of you with your thumb
   sticking up. Keep the rest of your hand in a fist.
3. Look at your thumb with both eyes and hold your head
   perfectly still. If necessary, ask a partner to hold your
   head or balance a book on your head to prevent uncon-
   scious rotation or bobbing.
4. Continue to look at your thumb as you rotate your arm
   in a circle about two feet in diameter. The center of the
   circle should be level with your nose.

5. To increase the level of difficulty, continue to look at your thumb as you rotate your arm in a large, horizontal figure eight, first with one hand and then the other. This should be a large figure. The center of the figure should be level with your nose; extend your arms as far as possible without straining the muscles of your eyes.
6. Then, rotate your arm in a cloverleaf pattern while you continue to follow your thumb with your eyes.

X Marks the Spot

Purpose of this Activity:
This activity helps students develop auditory sequencing memory (the ability to hear and recall words in order) and the ability to accurately aim the eye (Kimple, 1997). Auditory sequencing memory is used mainly to develop language and follow directions; eye-aiming accuracy is needed to read. The complexity of remembering and aiming in sequence simultaneously engages several neuronal networks in the visual and auditory systems. The more often these networks are activated, the more myelinated they become. The extreme muscle movements required by this exercise condition the six movement-control muscles of each eye so they can maintain strength and flexibility (Koslowe, 1995).

What to Do:
1. Stand approximately ten feet from a wall or other rectangular target. You should be able to see all four corners of the wall by moving only your eyes.
2. Without moving your head, look at the upper right-hand corner of the wall.

3. Move your eyes to look at different corners one at a time. (Try turning this into a game of Simon Says for young children or learners who have trouble following oral directions.)
4. To increase the difficulty of this exercise, lengthen the series of movements the eye makes before resting. For example, you might say, "You are now looking at the upper left-hand corner. Move your eyes to the upper right-hand corner and then keep moving your eyes until you get to the bottom right-hand corner." (When you give multi-step directions, it is often helpful for the students to repeat them aloud while acting on them.)

Variation:
Write your name on the wall with your eyes.

Eye Massage

Purpose of this Activity:
You'll notice that students' attentional behaviors change when they are experiencing eye distress. Visual functioning is a complex process. At least thirteen distinct vision-related skills are used continuously throughout the day, accounting for eighty to ninety percent of the information the brain receives at school (Cheatum & Hammond, 2000; Spache et al. 1992)! Eye muscle fatigue after seatwork can result in watering eyes, reddened eyes or complaints of headache. Perform an *Eye Massage* whenever you notice students displaying physical discomfort during or after reading or copying tasks.

What to Do:
This is a four-phase massage.

1. Use both thumbs to massage the inside corners of your eyes, beneath the eyebrows. Rest your fingers against the sides of your head.
2. Use your right thumb and forefinger to massage the bridge of your nose. Massage in a vertical, circular motion.
3. Use your index fingers to massage your cheeks about an inch away from your nose. Rest your thumbs beneath your chin.
4. Gently massage your eyebrows, eyes and the hollow below your eyes with the knuckles of your index and middle fingers. Massage from the center of the eyes outward. Rest your thumbs on each side of your forehead and curl the rest of your fingers in a relaxed fist.

Binocular Training

Materials Needed:
A book or handout to read; a standard 1" x 12" ruler

Purpose of this Activity:
Binocular vision, also known as fusion, is the eye's ability to take information from both eyes and fuse them into a single image in the brain. Binocular vision allows a wider field of vision and enables objects to be seen in three dimensions (depth perception). If the eyes do not meet at the same spot when they coordinate information, double vision often results. Without binocular vision, children tend to read with just one eye or to alternate reading from one eye to the other. As a consequence, they tend to lose or omit many words at the expense of comprehension (Kimple, 1997). *Binocular Training* encourages the use of both eyes and reduces the tendency to see with only one eye at a time.

What to Do:
1. Position the reading material about fifteen inches away from you.
2. Hold the ruler vertically near the reading material. Slowly move it towards you from where the reading material is to the point where the ruler appears to double when you are looking at the print. (You will be able to see "through"   the doubled ruler when you read.)
3. Begin to read the material, making sure to keep both eyes open. If the ruler blocks out words as you are reading, try blinking your eyes and see if the blocked word is visible. If that doesn't work, readjust the ruler slightly so that you can see the word.
4. Concentrate on seeing with both eyes.
5. Do this exercise for three to five minutes while reading your assigned material, resting your eyes when tired.

Letter Reading Boogie

Materials Needed:
A random string of letters or numbers displayed on an overhead projector; metronome (optional)

Purpose of this Activity:
The six eye muscles used for visual tracking connect to the top, sides and bottom of each eye, allowing it to move in all directions. These are the same muscles that hold the eye steady once it fixates upon a target. If the muscles of both eyes are not coordinated, any images they receive may be blurred or doubled (Spache et al., 1992). An activity like *Letter Reading Boogie* increases the tracking speed and accuracy of these eye-aiming muscles to make reading from the board easier and more efficient.

What to Do:
1. Write, without any spacing, a sequence of letters and or numbers in a line.
2. Have students read aloud, in unison, each letter, progressing from left to right.
3. Now, have students read each letter from right to left.
4. Have students read every other letter from left to right.
5. Have students read every third letter from left to right.
6. Repeat steps 2 through 5 while keeping a steady beat.

Variations:
1. Use numbers or long words instead of letters.
2. Have students read printed letters (from a typewriter or computer) instead of handwritten ones.

Bring It Into Focus

Materials Needed:
Pencil with letters, such as "No. 2" or a corporation name, stamped on it; far target of letters or numbers, such as a clock, poster or writing on the chalkboard

Purpose of this Activity:
Visual accommodation is the ability to keep your eyes focused when you move your gaze from a near target to a far target. Children need to be able to maintain their focus at board and desk distances, and change their focus easily. For some students, the focus mechanism may change too slowly, causing them to take more time than average to complete their work. This exercise increases the eye's ability to focus accurately and quickly when copying information from the board.

What to Do:

1. Stand in a relaxed posture with your weight equally distributed over both feet and your knees slightly bent.
2. Hold the pencil about six inches in front of your eyes while facing the far target. You should be able to see the letters on the pencil clearly.
3. Look first at the pencil, then at the far target, waiting until you see the letters clearly at one distance before looking at the other.
4. Repeat this sequence fifteen to twenty times as rapidly as your ability to focus your eyes allows.

Pencil Push-Ups

Materials Needed:
Pencil with letters, such as "No. 2" or a corporation name stamped on it

Purpose of this Activity:
As an object approaches your face, an increased demand is placed upon the eye muscles that help turn the eyes inward so that they can maintain a single, clear image of the target. Students' eyes rely on this process of convergence, or convergent accommodation, as they work at their desks. *Pencil Push-Ups* enhance their ability to aim and focus both of their eyes when they activate their near vision system.

What to Do:

1. Hold the pencil at eye level approximately twelve inches in front of your nose.
2. Look at a single letter on the pencil. Make sure the image stays in focus and does not double.

3. Move the pencil slowly toward your nose while keeping both of your eyes fixed on the target letter. If the letter doubles, your eyes are no longer accurately on target (one eye has slipped slightly). Move the pencil away from your nose until the letter becomes a single letter and reattempt to bring it toward your nose.
4. Repeat this exercise three to five times, keeping the image of the letter in focus and distinctly single.

Eye Muscle Tennis

Materials Needed:
Grade-level appropriate reading material

Purpose of this Activity:
The muscles used to track print from the board are the same ones used to read from a book. The size of the jumps the eye makes between fixations (focus points), however, is smaller when you read from a book; near reading requires a different level of muscle control. With practice, the ability of your eye to move smoothly across the page improves, increasing the pace at which you can read. *Eye Muscle Tennis* increases the tracking speed and accuracy of your eye-aiming muscles.

What to Do:
1. With the reading material in both hands, start at the top of the page and read the first and last *letter* of each line as fast as possible without making mistakes or getting lost.
2. Then, read the first and last letter of each line starting at the lower right-hand portion of the page and moving up.
3. To further increase the level of difficulty, walk as you read the letters.
4. Once you are able to read the letters quickly and accurately, walk and read the first and last *word* of each line. This activity may be difficult.

Manipulating Art and Science Tools: Activating the Fine Motor System for Production

The successful completion of a science experiment or an art project depends partly on competent manual dexterity. Giving students a chance to develop the fine motor muscles needed to manipulate tools and other equipment may help improve their academic functioning.

The cast of characters with fine motor dysfunction is easily recognized. Drindl Drop-A-Lot, who is forever chasing her flying utensil across the cafeteria. Izzy I-Can't-Draw, who avoids creative assignments and other graphic activities. Trevor Tripper, who never has his shoes tied. Henrietta Hunt-And-Peck, who cannot learn to type by touch no matter how hard she tries. In contrast to these students, children with effective fine motor function hold and use tools easily, draw shapes or figures well, tie their shoes, play an instrument and easily type on a keyboard.

Most likely, students with fine motor dysfunction have graphomotor challenges as well. Moving a pencil to write demands the coordination of muscles in the ends of our fingers to push it left and right, up and down, and in circles. This section contains simple exercises designed to strengthen the sub-skills needed to improve fine motor functioning and handwriting.

Symptoms of fine motor dysfunction include:
- poor desk posture
- avoidance of or difficulty with drawing and cutting
- inefficient grasp and manipulation of small utensils
- pencil lines that are weak and wobbly or tight and dark
- constantly broken pencil lead
- unclear establishment of hand dominance

Symptoms of graphomotor dysfunction include:
- difficulty copying from the board or overhead
- inconsistent letter formation
- slowness completing written assignments
- awkward or uncomfortable pencil grip

Transitioning to these Exercises

Hint: Explaining the reason for performing these exercises is just as important as telling students how to do them. For example, try this very brief introduction:

"Now, let's get our hands ready for the next task."

Hint: Perform these exercises throughout lessons that require an extensive use of the fine motor system.

Hint: Encourage students to perform these exercises during other classes, at home or whenever they feel like their hands need to rest or be strengthened.

Activities

Posture Check

Purpose of this Activity:
Students will sacrifice all forms of mobility for the sake of stability. To improve their concentration and enhance their ability to use fine motor skills while sitting, make sure that your students can answer "Yes" to each of these questions.

1. Are your hips, knees and feet bent at ninety-degree angles?
2. Are your feet on the floor?
3. Are your shoulders slightly pulled back, level and relaxed?

Note:
If some students' feet do not touch the floor, place a box or stool beneath their feet to help them maintain stability. You may also need to adjust the height of their desks or chairs to help them achieve optimal posture.

Puttin' on the Mitts

Purpose of this Activity:

Special receptors in our muscles tell the brain where a certain body part is located in space. These receptors also respond to directions from the brain to control the muscles needed for a particular task. They are the communicators that assist with praxis, the ability to plan, organize and complete a series of movements directed toward a purpose (Cheatum & Hammond, 2000). Physically stimulating

these muscles with deep pressure initiates the praxis system used for writing or creating things (like a collage or sculpture) with the fingers and hands.

What to Do:

1. Wake up the muscle communication cells in the upper body by using an open hand to heavily pat your arm from the fingertips to the shoulder joint. Pat each arm two times.
2. Put an imaginary glove on one hand. With one hand, apply deep pressure to the fingers of the other hand (one at a time). Switch hands.

Variations:

1. Slowly apply hand lotion to individual fingers.
2. Poke or push individual fingers through clay or playing dough.

Cut-Ups

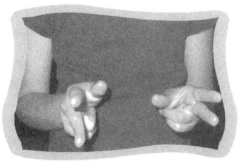

Purpose of this Activity:
Using scissors in a precise manner is a very difficult task to master. Cutting is the one of the most complex skills demanded of the grasping muscle system in the hands. Furthermore, the movements that enable you to cut are the same movements that enable you to perform a wide variety of other activities, including picking up and holding onto small items, manipulating knobs, buttoning clothing and playing musical instruments (Smits-Engelsman et al., 2001). Although students with a poor grasping system are not doomed to an academic career of failure, they do tend to drop items or otherwise appear to be "all thumbs," as the saying goes (Schneider, 2001)! *Cut-Ups* maneuvers strengthen the open-close grasp needed for easily executing the fine motor movements that help you create new objects and manipulate small equipment.

What to Do:
If possible, perform these movements with both hands simultaneously. If not, start with just the writing hand and add the other hand later.
1. Open and close your hands ten times. Hyperextend your fingers as you open and make a tight fist as you close.
2. Snap your fingers four times.
3. Fold your pinky finger and ring finger onto the palm of the hand, leaving the thumb, index and middle finger—the scissor-holding fingers—extended.
4. Open and close your scissor fingers ten times while leaving the other two fingers against the palms.
5. Shake out your hands to relax them.

Double Duty

Materials Needed:
Pencil

Purpose of this Activity:
Reviewing materials can be a dry task, but practice and drill is a very important component of automatically knowing math facts, high frequency words or spelling patterns. Adding a sensory experience to the recitation of the math facts table engages a greater number of sensory systems, which creates more paths for accessing these facts (Jensen, 2000a). With more pathways to travel in the brain, these skills will come automatically, freeing students from the need to slow down to add something on paper or decode words sound by sound (Levine, 2003).

What to Do:
1. In the air, draw spelling words or answers to review questions while properly gripping a pencil.
2. Use hand and finger shadows during an oral presentation.
3. Teach sign language letters and practice spelling vocabulary words.

Pencil Tricks

Materials Needed:
Pencil

Purpose of this Activity:
The development of the fine motor muscles used for writing occurs in early childhood when we play board games, shuffle cards or assemble jigsaw puzzles. Finger painting, playing with dough and sewing activities provide in early childhood

the much-needed tactile information fingers will later use in
school to make models, type on
keyboards and manipulate lab
equipment in science class. With
today's ever-increasing emphasis
on electronics and technology,
games and handcrafts are not
paid much attention anymore.
Thus for many children, the fine
motor muscles in their hands do
not develop sufficiently. *Pencil
Tricks* will help isolate and
strengthen specific muscle sets to
help students bring up to speed
the fine motor development in
their hands that may be delayed.

What to Do:
At first, perform all of these exercises with just your writing hand.
Once your writing hand has mastered the exercises, try them with
the other hand.

1. Roll the pencil from the tips of
   your fingers to the center of
   your palm and all the way back.
2. Walk your fingers up and down the pencil using a tripod
   grasp.
3. Turn the pencil end over end by using only the fingers of
   one hand.

Variation:
Recite math facts or practice spelling words while performing any of the exercises above.

Get a Grip on Handwriting Skills

Materials Needed:
Pencil

Purpose of this Activity:
Inappropriate pencil grasps can result in a slower writing rate, muscle fatigue and the avoidance of writing tasks in general. Building strength in the fine muscles used for writing, as well as improving students' pencil grip, will increase their stamina for writing (Graham et al., 2000). As with any skill, practice makes perfect—even the most accomplished writers in your class will benefit from a reminder to relax and check their writing grip when you ask a question like, "Is everyone 'OK' to write?"

What to Do:
1. Make an "OK" sign while grasping the pencil with your thumb, index and third fingers.
2. Model to your class three types of efficient grips. As long as the students can keep their hand in a relaxed "OK" sign while they write, their grip is efficient.

Tripod grasp—Hold the pencil with the tip of your thumb and index finger and rest the pencil point against the fingertip of your middle finger. The thumb and index finger form a circle.

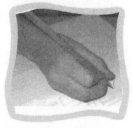

Adaptive tripod grasp—Hold the pencil between the index and third fingers with the tips of the thumb and index finger on the pencil. The pencil rests against the side of the third finger near the first knuckle.

Quadrupod grasp—Hold the pencil with the tip of the thumb, index finger and middle finger. The pencil point rests against the fingertip of the ring finger.

A list of common handwriting problems and suggested solutions can be found in the Appendix on page 120.

6 Getting Started: Designing Your Own Sequences

Some Examples to Help You Get Started

The purpose of this chapter is to
present simple exercises in an
easy-to-use format for teachers who want to incorporate
sensory development into their
lesson plans. These sample REAL
transitions are listed by subject area to help
get you started. There is nothing extraordi-
nary or magical about these examples; I
encourage you to substitute other
Sensorcises in place of activities that may
not be appropriate for your classroom.
These models are provided for the sole
purpose of easing the burden of planning
from your shoulders. They represent just
a few of the many possible combinations
you could create for any subject. Included are
charts and scripts for seven different subject areas and common school events: reading, writing, mathematics, science,

physical education, assemblies and test taking. They are listed in order by their likeliness to occur in your curriculum, from daily lessons to occasional events.

When you first implement the *Sensorcises* program, choose one of these subject areas to practice with and commit to making those exercises a habit for you and your students. The subject area's accompanying chart will show you a possible sequence of activities, with the activity names, page numbers to find them, materials and space required, and brief descriptions to refresh your memory. Directly following the table are sample scripts you can use to focus your students and explain to them an activity's purpose. You may use any of these exercises in isolation throughout the day.

Although they are obvious to most teachers, there are two more points worth mentioning: model every step and never give more than two steps of directions at one time. Lastly... have fun!

Before Reading

Exercise Category	Name	Page	Materials & Prep	Space Needed	Exercise Description
Relax the stress response system	*Push Through Barriers*	20	none	chair, desk or wall to push on	lengthening the calf muscles
Energize cellular communication	*Drink Water*	35	water bottles	sitting or standing	drinking water
Activate large muscles for optimal learning	*Whirling and Twirling*	52	none	adequate space for extended arms and body rotations	spinning around with arms extended
Lead "sense"-ibly into learning	*Head Turners and Thumbs Up*	82 & 83	none	sitting or standing	eye muscle movements to improve tracking

What to Say

Push Through Barriers

"Before we start our reading today, I want you to get a drink of water and begin to loosen the tension in your body with a calf stretch that looks like this...." (You demonstrate the calf stretch.) "Stretch until both of your legs are relaxed and limber."

Drink Water

"Our brains need water to function efficiently. Take another swallow or two of water from your bottle."

Whirling and Twirling

"One of the ways to plug in the brain is to spin in circles. Find yourself some space by your desk that's big enough to turn around in a full circle without bumping into someone or something. Great! Ready? Put your arms out and spin as fast as you can comfortably until I say, 'stop.' Start spinning! Find a target to focus on each time you turn around and keep your head level.... Stop! Stay standing but close your eyes so that the only thing you are focused on is standing still and regaining your sense of equilibrium. Now, open your eyes, raise your arms and spin as fast as is comfortable in the other direction until I say, 'stop....' Stop! Stay standing and close your eyes again. Please take your seats."

(The first few times you perform this activity with your class, have them spin only for a brief interval. Gradually increase the length of time you have them spin until you reach a maximum of two minutes. Likewise, when they pause to rest after spins, gradually decrease the time until you have students standing still for only fifteen seconds.)

Head Turners
"Let's prepare the muscles of our eyes for our next lesson. Find something far away but at eye level and look at it. Lock it into your field of vision. Move your head as far as you can to the left, right, up, down and in circles while still looking at this target. If your eyes hurt, stop for a moment to rest and start again when you can."

Thumbs Up
"Our last exercise will strengthen our eyes. Make a fist with your thumb sticking up and put your arm straight out in front of you. This time we are going to lock our heads in place and move our eyes around. Slowly bring your thumb up, down, to the left, to the right, back and forth and in circles, following it the whole time with just your eyes—don't move your head! Again, if your eyes get tired or start to hurt, rest for a moment and begin again when you can."

Before Writing

Exercise Category	Name	Page	Materials & Prep	Space Needed	Exercise Description
Relax the stress response system	Fly Free	19	none	sitting or standing	upper body stretching
Energize cellular communication	Heart Smart	36	none	sitting or standing	breathing and focused thought
Activate large muscles for optimal learning	Cross Overs	53	none	space for each student to stand arm's length apart	leg and arm exercises
Lead "sense"-ibly into learning	Puttin' on the Mitts	94	none	sitting or standing	finger exercise

What to Say

Fly Free

"Before we start our writing today, let's take a short break to prepare our body and brain for it. Stand up and raise your arms straight above your head. Reach for the sky with your right hand; reach with your left hand. Now, with your right hand, reach across the top of your head and gently pull your left elbow towards your left ear. Breathe slowly."

(Have students hold this posture for ten seconds and then switch arms.)

Heart Smart

"Okay. Let's put our arms down but keep taking deep breaths. Place both hands over your heart and imagine that you are breathing through this part of your chest. Close your eyes and focus on something in your life that makes you very happy."

(Have students hold this posture and breathing pattern for thirty seconds—more if they really need it.)

Cross Overs

"Everyone, open your eyes; find your balance and slowly raise your right knee up to touch your left elbow. Hold this position. Now, slowly drop your leg and move your arm to its normal place. Raise your left knee to touch your right elbow in the same way. Do several sets of these as slowly as you can.... Please take your seats."

(Have students do five to ten sets of this exercise.)

Puttin' on the Mitts

"Fingers have special muscles that need exercise, too. Imagine that you have a pair of heavy gloves. Slowly slide them on one finger at a time, as you squeeze and apply deep pressure with one hand to the fingers of the other. When you have put the 'glove' on one hand and massaged each of the fingers, switch to massage the other hand. Our lesson today will focus on writing good paragraphs. As we review the elements of a well-structured, complete paragraph, continue with your finger massage."

Before Math

Exercise Category	Name	Page	Materials & Prep	Space Needed	Exercise Description
Relax the stress response system	*Release Pressure Points*	22	none	standing room	acupressure point manipulation
Energize cellular communication	*Hook Up to Rewire Your Emotions*	37	none	sitting or standing	cross-body stretch and breathing
Activate large muscles for optimal learning	*Lateral Tapping*	54	teacher needs a metronome or pencil to tap loudly	sitting, standing or floor exercises	arm, leg, hand & foot patterning exercises
Lead "sense"-ibly into learning	*Pencil Tricks*	96	posted review materials; learners need pencils	sitting or standing	pencil twirling and fact review

What to Say

Release Pressure Points
"I need you to stand up so we can get ready for math. There are special places in our body that collect tension during the day. Right now we are going to find the ones on our legs and release it. Drop your arms at your sides and use your longest finger to find the tender spot on each thigh. Rub it with your fingertips until the tenderness disappears or lessens."

Hook Up to Rewire Your Emotions

"The next thing we need to do is clear our circuits so our cells can better communicate with each other. There are several steps to this exercise. Here's step one: Stand in place and cross your legs at the ankles. Good. Now, extend your arms in front of you and put your hands together as if you were going to clap. Pretend you missed and cross your arms at the wrists. Turn your palms to face each other and lace your fingers together. Pull your clasped hands toward your heart and rest your pinky fingers against your chest. Finally, relax your tongue on the roof of your mouth and breathe calmly (for thirty seconds or more). Ok, uncross your arms and legs, stand with your feet shoulder-width apart, clasp your hands normally and bring them to rest above your heart. Breathe with your tongue at the roof of your mouth like before (for another thirty seconds or more). Now that our bodies are prepared, we can get the right and left hemispheres of our brain working together. Have a seat for the last exercise."

Lateral Tapping

"I am going to stomp my feet and slap parts of my body to create a pattern. Watch and listen." (Tap out your pattern and name the body parts and actions as you do so.) "I will continue this pattern and I would like you to join in when you are ready." (Wait until all the students are following along, and then stop calling out body parts—but don't stop the rhythm.) "Let's keep a steady beat going as we count by threes to the number thirty. Ready to count? Here we go! Three, six, nine, twelve, ...thirty. Good. Please take out your pencils."

Pencil Tricks

"Hold your pencil with your writing hand and twirl it through your fingers as we count by fours from zero to sixty."

Before Science

Exercise Category	Name	Page	Materials & Prep	Space Needed	Exercise Description
Relax the stress response system	*Lighten the Brain Stem's Heavy Load*	23	none	standing room	neck stretches
Energize cellular communication	*Lymphatic Flush*	38	none	standing room	pressure point
Activate large muscles for optimal learning	*Don't Rock the Boat!*	56	none	standing room	balancing activity
Lead "sense"-ibly into learning	*Cut-Ups*	95	none	sitting or standing	fine motor warm-up

What to Say

Lighten the Brain Stem's Heavy Load

"Before we begin our science lesson, let's prepare our body and mind for learning. We all carry stress in the neck, near our brain stem. We can release some tension from that area and give our brain stems a chance to rest. Relax your arms naturally at your sides and allow your left ear to gently fall toward your left shoulder. Stop when you feel the muscles tighten—don't force them—and lift your head back to center. Now, gently drop your right ear. Good. Let your left ear fall toward your left shoulder again, but this time, put your right arm behind your back as you do so. Hold this position (for thirty seconds) and breathe deeply. Switch sides and hold the position again. We'll finish by gently dropping our head to our chest and smoothly rolling our head in semi-circles. Do not roll your neck completely around! There are many fine nerve endings on the back of your neck and head that you could pinch or hurt."

Lymphatic Flush

"In our bodies, above the arteries carrying our blood, are special points; rubbing them helps clear the electrical system of the body for learning. With one hand, find two points in the hollows just below your collarbone on either side of your breastbone. Place your thumb on one side and two fingers on the other and massage the tension away from these points. With your other hand, cover your belly button and breathe deeply."

(Have students massage their collarbone points for one to two minutes while they keep the other hand in place.)

Don't Rock the Boat!

"Our balancing system helps us stay seated and hold science equipment steady. We need to balance ourselves before we move on today. Stand with your feet slightly spread apart. Practice balancing by raising one foot—keep your legs straight—about ten inches from the floor and hold the position for a minimum of five seconds. Switch feet. Next, balance on one foot and swing the other leg back and forth ten times, then switch feet."

(Have students repeat either balance with their eyes closed. This will demonstrate the effect that vision plays in balancing. To further increase the level of difficulty, have them try to rotate their eyes beneath the eyelids while performing the activity.)

Cut-Ups

"Let's prepare our hands to handle our science equipment. Open and close your hands ten times. Snap your fingers four times. Fold your pinky finger and ring finger onto the palm of your hand, leaving your thumb and other two fingers—your scissor holders—free to open and close. Open and close your scissor holders ten times and then shake out your hands."

(Have students perform these movements with both hands simultaneously, if possible. If not, start with the writing hand and add the other one later.)

Before P. E.

Exercise Category	Name	Page	Materials & Prep	Space Needed	Exercise Description
Relax the stress response system	*The Brain Wiggle*	24	none	squad spots on the floor or ground	seated tailbone stimulation
Energize cellular communication	*Drink Water*	35	water bottles or nearby drinking fountain	sitting or standing	drinking water
Activate large muscles for optimal learning	*Crazy Eights*	58	none	gymnasium or room of similar size	follow the leader in a large figure eight pattern
Lead "sense"-ibly into learning	any tossing and catching activity	N/A	things to toss and catch	gymnasium or room of similar size	tossing and catching

What to Say

The Brain Wiggle
"After sitting for long periods of time, tension builds up in our tailbone. Let's loosen the vertebrae there. Sit on the floor and place both hands behind your hips with your fingertips pointing forward. Lift your feet off the floor and rock back and forth on your tailbone in small circles until you feel less tense."

(Students can also perform this activity while sitting in chairs during an academic lesson.)

Drink Water
At frequent intervals, remind your students to drink water to refresh themselves.

Crazy Eights
"Today we will walk in a figure eight pattern for our moving warm-up. I'll outline the shape on the floor and you will follow me through it." (Make the pattern large enough for

everyone in the group to follow you without bumping into each other.) "As we walk, make sure your arms and legs are moving opposite of each other. Good. Please return to your squad spots to hear the directions for our next activity."

Tossing and Catching Activity
Play any tossing and catching game or practice drills that are suitable for your physical education curriculum. See page 125 for some examples.

Before Assemblies

Exercise Category	Name	Page	Materials & Prep	Space Needed	Exercise Description
Relax the stress response system	*Seated Toe Touches*	25	none	sitting or standing	stretches
Energize cellular communication	*Chill Out*	43	none	sitting or standing	breathing exercise
Activate large muscles for optimal learning	*Wake Up the Little Brain*	57	none	sitting room	large muscle stimulation
Lead "sense"-ibly into learning	*Ear Lobe Roll*	69	none	sitting room	ear lobe manipulation

What to Say

Seated Toe Touches
"Before we go to the assembly, let's make ourselves relaxed, alert and focused. Sit comfortably and cross your feet at the ankles. Slowly reach for your ankles and let gravity pull you down. Drop your head and take a deep breath. Hold it; gently exhale as you reach towards your toes three times. Now, recross your legs so the other ankle is on top and repeat this exercise."

Chill Out

"Now we need to cool and calm our brains! Relax your tongue against the roof of your mouth. Press your right nostril shut and inhale through the left. Take five deep breaths through the left nostril. Now press your left nostril shut and take five deep breaths through the right. Repeat the activity to give each nostril a minimum of two sets of breathing turns."

Wake Up the Little Brain

"Let's continue with five chair lift-ups. Put your hands on your chair under your thighs. Push down to lift your bottom off the seat. Slowly lower yourself down and lift yourself up again. Lift slowly and fluidly to give your muscles a good work out!"

Ear Lobe Roll

"Finally, we need to prepare our ears for listening. Use your thumbs and forefingers to gently roll and unroll the cartilage at the edge of each ear. Start at the top and move down to the fleshy lobe. When you get to the bottom, change directions."

(Have students perform this ear massage on both ears simultaneously for about one minute.)

Before a Test

Exercise Category	Name	Page	Materials & Prep	Space Needed	Exercise Description
Relax the stress response system	Stretch the Jaw Joint	26	none	sitting or standing	yawning to intake oxygen and reduce jaw muscle tension
Energize cellular communication	Sweep Away Stress	41	none	sitting or standing	eye rotations
Activate large muscles for optimal learning	Don't Rock the Boat!	56	none	standing room	balancing while standing
Lead "sense"-ibly into learning	Posture Check	93	none	sitting room	check for optimum posture for desk work

What to Say

Stretch the Jaw Joint

"As you know, today is the social studies test we have been preparing for. How many of you are a little nervous? That's to be expected. We can help your brain and body relax with a few simple exercises. First, pretend to yawn. Put your fingertips against any tight spots you feel on your jaw; make a deep, relaxed, yawning sound while you ease away all the tension, starting at the chin and gently stroking along the jaw line up to your ears, temples, across your forehead and above the eyebrows. Increase the pressure of this massage as much as you can tolerate."

Sweep Away Stress

"Next, let's release some stress and energize our brain cells to help us remember things better. Find the most tender points right above the eyebrows on both sides of your forehead. Gently pull up on the tissue and hold it while we perform the next part of the activity. Ready? Slowly rotate your eyes once clockwise and then once counterclockwise. Go slightly past your starting point when you change directions. Repeat these circles until your eyes rotate smoothly. As you perform this activity, mentally motivate yourselves to do well on this test with positive thoughts like, 'I am calm and ready to show what I know.'"

Don't Rock the Boat!

"Keep those positive thoughts going! Now, stand up and try to remember the key points we reviewed yesterday. Balance yourselves on one foot; switch feet. Good. Take a few swallows from your water bottle and sit down."

Posture Check

"The best way to stay relaxed during this test is to maintain good posture. Let's do a posture check now. Are your hips, knees and feet at a ninety-degree angles? Are your feet solid on the floor? Are your shoulders relaxed and facing forward?"

How to Design Your Own Sequences

Sensorcises are easy to fit into your daily routine. Any time your class changes subjects, include in your transition plan a specific series of exercises to promote the optimal brain functioning needed for the lesson to come. Follow these steps to get in the habit of using Sensorcises regularly.

1. Hang a poster of the word REAL at the back part of your teaching area as a visual reminder of the REAL sequence. Make sure it is in a place where you cannot miss seeing it.
2. Find a subject you know you will be teaching almost daily.
3. Put together a routine that will support the skills needed for the subject you selected. (The sample transitions from the previous section should give you some ideas.)
4. Teach the exercises to your students. Start with just one activity from the sequence (maybe the one for *Relax*) and practice it daily before the beginning of a lesson until you or the students tire of it. Then, teach another activity from the sequence until students know all four exercises. Practice daily.
5. Begin combining two or more of the activities and work up to the complete sequence.
6. Once your class has mastered the first routine, add a second to the daily schedule.

The following table summarizes the Sensorcises that you could choose from for a variety of subject areas or school experiences. As you work with these formal transitions, you will begin to notice other times during a lesson when learners could use a brief change of pace. You can even use Sensorcises as sponge activities or for unscheduled detours when you need to get your students back on track. By varying the routines regularly, you will become more proficient at recalling some of the specific exercises from this book, until finally you are able to improvise.

Comprehensive List of Activities

	Page #	Reading	Writing	Math	Science	Social Studies & Health	P. E.	Computer Lab	Assemblies	Test Taking & Quiet Study
Relax										
Fly Free	19	•	•	•	•	•	•	•	•	•
Push Through Barriers	20	•	•	•	•	•	•	•		•
Desk Breathing	21	•	•	•	•	•				•
Release Pressure Points	22	•	•	•	•	•	•	•	•	•
Lighten the Brain Stem's Heavy Load	23	•	•	•	•	•	•	•	•	•
The Brain Wiggle	24	•	•	•	•	•	•	•	•	•
Seated Toe Touches	25	•	•	•	•	•		•		•
Stretch the Jaw Joint	26	•	•	•	•	•		•	•	•
Energize Cellular Communication										
Drink Water	35	•	•	•	•	•	•	•	•	•
Heart Smart	36	•	•	•	•	•	•	•	•	•
Hook Up to Rewire Your Emotions	37	•	•	•	•	•	•	•	•	•
Lymphatic Flush	38	•	•	•	•	•	•	•	•	•
Block Buster	39	•	•	•	•	•		•	•	•
Sweep Away Stress	41	•	•	•	•	•		•	•	•
Chill Out	43	•	•	•	•	•		•	•	•
Activate Large Muscles for Optimal Learning										
Whirling and Twirling	52	•	•	•	•	•	•	•		•
Cross Overs	53	•	•	•	•	•	•	•	•	•
Lateral Tapping	54	•	•	•	•	•		•		•
Don't Rock the Boat!	56	•	•	•	•	•	•	•	•	•
Wake Up the Little Brain	57	•	•	•	•	•		•		•
Crazy Eights	58	•	•	•	•	•	•			•
Lead "Sense"-ibly										
Listening and Communication										
Ear Lobe Roll	69	•				•			•	
Repeat After Me	70		•	•				•	•	
Memory Stretcher	71		•	•	•	•		•	•	
Dot-Dot-Dash	72		•	•	•			•		

Comprehensive List of Activities
continued

	Page #	Reading	Writing	Math	Science	Social Studies & Health	P. E.	Computer Lab	Assemblies	Test Taking & Quiet Study
Reading and Writing										
Visualizations to Improve Reading Comprehension	77	•								
Visualizations to Improve Writing	78		•							
Creative Visualizations for Solving Problems	80		•	•						•
Tracking, Copying and Eye Muscle Control										
Head Turners	82	•	•	•	•	•				•
Thumbs Up	83	•	•	•	•	•				•
X Marks the Spot	84	•	•	•	•	•		•		•
Eye Massage	85	•	•	•	•	•		•	•	•
Binocular Training	86	•	•	•	•	•		•	•	•
Letter Reading Boogie	87	•	•	•	•	•				•
Bring It into Focus	88	•	•	•	•	•		•	•	•
Pencil Push-Ups	89	•	•	•	•	•				•
Eye Muscle Tennis	90	•	•	•	•	•		•		•
Manipulating Arts and Science Tools										
Posture Check	93	•	•	•	•	•		•		•
Puttin' on the Mitts	94		•	•	•	•		•		•
Cut-Ups	95		•	•	•	•		•		•
Double Duty	96		•	•	•	•				
Pencil Tricks	96		•	•	•	•				•
Get a Grip on Handwriting Skills	98		•	•	•	•				•

In Conclusion

Learning is a sensory experience. Whether we are reading silently, composing our thoughts for writing or learning to play an instrument in music class, the information we work with is received through the sensory system, processed in the brain and sent out for some sort of eventual or immediate motor response. After reading this book, you may wonder if the students you always thought had behavior problems are simply responding with poor sensory development and integration to events in their life. Or, if students you thought had poor work habits are actually unable to use their motor skills to produce the kind of work they are asked to do. These are the kinds of thoughts and questions I hope to evoke. A long time ago, a professor told me, "Behavior is purposeful!" I am sure many of you think that statement is too obvious to be significant. But for me, this concept completely changed my way of understanding people, especially the children in my charge. Instead of assuming some children were mischievous, lazy or inattentive, I became curious about what their behavior could tell me about their needs as learners: Are they tired from sitting still? Are they thirsty? Do they need me to present this concept in another way? Should I modify this activity?

Children (all people, really) will telegraph their physical needs to you. As you practice these sensory exercises with them, you will start to interpret their behavior and performance as physical telegraphs and notice times when your entire class could use a stretch or practice with some specific sensory function. That will be your cue to perform one or two Sensorcises before advancing to the next lesson. Of course, no learning or behavior problem can be completely overcome with a one-minute exercise break, but if you take the time to observe your students and respond to the physical cues they send you, I think you will be pleasantly surprised by the results.

Appendix

Planning Template for Your Own REAL Transition Routines

Create your own formal transition plans with this template. Eventually, you'll have a set of REAL transition plans for your most common areas of instruction. Include a copy with your substitute teacher plans, too.

Exercise Category	Name	Page	Materials & Prep	Space Needed	Exercise Description
Relax the stress response system					
Energize cellular communication					
Activate large muscles for optimal learning					
Lead "Sense"-ibly into learning					

Common Handwriting Problems and Solutions

Student moves arms and shoulders while writing: Have the child lie on the floor to write. This position puts weight on her arms and stabilizes them. You could also have her write on a vertical surface like a chalkboard or easel, which helps the child's wrists hold a functional writing position as well as condition her shoulder stability.

Student does not put space between words: Give the child a stamp pad so he can stamp his fingerprint between each word. Gradually, eliminate the ink from practice lessons and have the child measure one finger-space to separate words. As he develops a better understanding of the concept of space between words, he will naturally stop using his finger.

Student grips the pencil too hard: Have the child practice coloring with a pencil a series of small shapes light gray, medium gray, dark gray and black to increase her awareness of different degrees of pressure on the pencil. Use a mechanical pencil so she learns to control how much pressure she puts on it; mechanical pencil points break very easily and provide immediate feedback to the student. If problems persist, place her paper on a phone book or writing tablet to absorb some of the pressure as she writes and to remind her keep her hand relaxed.

Student grips the pencil too softly: Have the child practice coloring small shapes dark gray and black with his pencil. (You can sometimes solve this problem by correcting the pencil grasp of students who grip the pencil with too much hesitation or without any strength.)

Student has poor paper placement: Beginners (learning to print letters and words) should place their paper straight up and down (not tilted) so that they can focus on the letter formation as they observe it in print. Experienced printers (able to print sentences across the page) should place their paper at a slight angle to follow the natural arc of their writing hand. An angled paper helps a writer exert less effort when writing all the way across a page. For right-handed children, tilt the right-hand corners higher than the left; for left-handed children, tilt the left-hand corners higher than the right. Remind them to keep their writing hand below the line of writing to encourage a correct, neutral wrist position.

Student does not stabilize the paper with the other hand: Use a clipboard or a piece of tape to hold the child's paper in place until she develops fine motor skills in the fingers. By the time she reaches middle school, her handwriting process will be more automatic and require less purposeful, conscious movement. Once she has learned to easily and consistently form letters and words, she can practice the added skill of stabilizing the paper with her free hand by using the clipboard less and less often.

Student holds the pencil too close or too far from the tip: Wrap a small rubber band around the part of the pencil where a child should place his fingers. This will remind him where to hold the pencil. (On standard wooden pencils, this place is where the paint ends.)

Quick and Easy Activities for Any Classroom—No Special Tools Required!

Here is a partial list of sensory-building activities that were not included in the *Sensorcises* REAL sequence chapters because they either require more materials or take longer than a few minutes to complete. Use them as free time choices or incorporate them into your lessons and units.

Chalkboard Activities

These activities can be performed in small groups or as free time options. They build hand-eye coordination, visual planning skills and fine motor skills.

Mirror Writing—Draw a line down the center of the chalkboard. With a piece of chalk in each hand, simultaneously draw mirror images of a chosen design. You might start with a tree by having a student hold the chalk waist-high on either side of the dividing line and draw the base of the tree by swinging both hands out in a straight line and bringing them back again in an arch. Continue to the top, adding branches and leaves as the exercise continues.

Shape Tracing—Draw a series of circular and semicircular shapes on the board. Have a student step as close to the board as possible while still seeing the shapes' edges in periphery. Give the student a piece of chalk and have him trace over the shapes, drawing smooth lines without lifting the chalk.

Car Races—Place two pieces of chalk in a five-line chalk holder and draw wavy lines across the board. Give students a piece of chalk and have them "race" across the board with it. With smooth, continuous movement, they try to draw a third line between the two wavy ones, right in the middle of the road. Start with a wide road and narrow it as students master this skill. You can make it even more challenging by drawing sharp, jagged lines like mountain peaks.

Going in Circles—It is easier for children struggling with handwriting to learn to draw lines while standing at a chalkboard and making full arm swings. Have students begin this activity by making large circles with one hand at a time and then with both hands together. Decrease the diameter of the circles until the students' fingers take over the work of drawing and the hands stay still.

Worksheets that Work
When it makes sense to support learning with a worksheet, use one of the following types to enhance both academic and sensory skills. Keep a stack of these on hand for students who finish early, or as impromptu extra credit assignments.

Worksheet Type	Sensory Skills
word searches	visual tracking; visual closure (used in reading—seeing *part* of a word and making a reasonable guess about the *whole* word); hand-eye coordination
mazes	visual tracking; hand-eye coordination
anagrams (scrambled words)	visualization
dot-to-dots	hand-eye coordination; visual searching
symmetry drawing exercises	visualization; hand-eye coordination
hidden pictures	visual discrimination (finding a specific shape in the midst of a variety of other visual images)
tracing	hand-eye coordination; graphomotor skills
handwriting practice sheets	graphomotor skills
crossword puzzles	visual closure (used in reading—seeing *part* of a word and making a reasonable guess about the *whole* word)

Cutting Activities
Mastering the use of scissors takes practice, practice, practice! Try one of these activities within a curriculum-related project or as a free time choice.

Collage—As stand-alone art projects or curriculum-related assignments, cut-and-paste activities hit the mark. They are especially appropriate as final projects for any unit or study of a novel.

Spiral Springs—On any shape of paper, draw a line in concentric fashion and cut along it to the center. Hang the springs from the ceiling as decorations. Younger students should start with spiral lines spaced far apart. To make the activity more challenging, use a shape with several sides and space the lines very close together.

Recycled Learning—Cut up heavy materials like disposable pie tins, tag board or old playing cards to use in art projects or models that demonstrate learning after a unit.

Snip and Wear—Cut up colorful straws as beads for stringing into jewelry or classroom decorations.

Modeling with Clay
Activities with modeling clay strengthen the fine motor skills of the hands.

Clay Writing—During reading or language arts lessons, use modeling clay to spell out tricky words. With younger children, use clay for activities like memorizing their home phone numbers or spelling their last name. (Roll the clay into a snake to form the letters and numbers.)

3-D Math—Use clay and toothpicks to build geometric shapes during math. Experiment with both flat and three-dimensional shapes.

Clay Cycles—Use clay to represent aspects of a process; for example, a science class could illustrate with clay the life-cycle or how plants turn sunlight into energy.

Map It Out—Take advantage of the pliable nature of clay to represent topographical structures and local geography of regions studied during Social Studies classes.

Tossing and Catching

Introduce one of these games into your classroom routine to develop and improve student hand-eye coordination. Keep a selection of small balls and beanbags handy. Large sheets of newspaper crumpled into balls also work well.

Catch, You're It!—Toss a small ball or bean bag during review games, circle time or during a game of Quiet Ball at recess.

Up in the Air—Have students toss and catch a bean bag while reviewing math facts, spelling words or other factual information. Control the game by having students stand up and toss the ball so it can be caught at a level between the waist and eyebrows. The trick is to improve peripheral vision by keeping the eyes looking forward at the review or drill material, not following the trajectory of the bean bag.

Math Games
Games like these for math assignments or as activity choices will reinforce mathematical thinking, most of which is visual.

Math Game	Sensory Skills
tangrams	visual closure (seeing *part* and making a reasonable guess about the *whole*); visual memory; visualization
patterning block puzzles	visual closure (seeing *part* and making a reasonable guess about the *whole*); visual memory; visualization
geoboard challenges	finger dexterity; visual focusing; visualization
dominos math (use common dominos for addition or subtraction problems; enlarge domino tiles on paper as flashcards for learning math facts)	visual memory

Arts & Crafts
Arts and crafts activities can be used as projects to demonstrate learning within a subject area, as stand-alone art projects or as free time choices.

Activity	Sensory Skill
curling paper to make sculptures or cards	fine motor muscle development in the hands; manual dexterity
stitchery samplers (use yarn, burlap and needles to create a wall hanging that involves a variety of stitches and knots)	fine motor muscle development in the hands; manual dexterity; visual and motor planning; hand-eye coordination
paints of all kinds with brushes, fingers or sponges	hand-eye coordination; visualization skills
beading activities	hand-eye coordination
tracing activities with different stencils and patterns	hand-eye coordination
paper punching (use a pin to make holes in paper in the outline of desired shape; frame with popsicle sticks and display in a window so light shines through the holes)	fine motor muscle development in the hands; manual dexterity; visual and motor planning; hand-eye coordination

***Rainy Day Recess or Free Time Games
(Garage Sale Bargains)***

The games below develop the hand-eye coordination system and visual and motor planning, as well as higher level problem-solving skills like memory, mental imagery manipulation and hypothesis testing in a non-graded, fun way.

- puzzles
- jacks
- card games like Spit, Slap Jack and Concentration
- construction toys like *Lincoln Logs*, *Lego* bricks, *Bristle Blocks* and wooden blocks
- board games like chess or checkers

For Further Reading

To better understand the basics of applied brain science, try...

- Jensen, Eric (2000). *Brain Based Learning (Revised)*. Thousand Oaks: Corwin Press.
- Marzano, R., Pickering, D., & Pollock, J. (2001). *Classroom Instruction that Works: Research-Based Strategies for Increasing Student Achievement*. Alexandria, VA: Association for Supervision and Curriculum Development (ACSD).
- Amen, Daniel (1998). *Change Your Brain, Change Your Life*. New York, NY: Times Books/Random House.
- Robbins, Jim (2000). *A Symphony in the Brain: The Evolution of the New Brain Wave Biofeedback*. New York, NY: Grove Press.
- Hannaford, Carla (1995). *Smart Moves: Why Learning is Not All in Your Head*. Arlington, VA: Great Ocean Publishers.
- Bransford, J., Brown, A. & Cocking, R., (Eds.) (2000). *How People Learn: Brain, Mind, Experience, and School—Expanded Edition*. Washington, DC: National Academy Press.

For more information about sensory integration and learning, try...

- Cheatum, B. & Hammond, A. (2000). *Physical Activities for Improving Children's Learning and Behavior: A Guide to Sensory Motor Development.* Champaign, IL: Human Kinetics.
- Kranowitz, C. S. (2003). *The Out-of-Sync Child Has Fun: Activities for Kids with Sensory Integration Dysfunction.* New York, NY: Perigee.
- Promislow, Sharon (2000). *Making the Brain/Body Connection.* West Vancouver, BC: Kinetic Publishing.
- Goddard, Sally (1996). *A Teacher's Window into the Child's Mind and Papers from the Institute for Neuro-Physiological Psychology.* Eugene, OR: Fern Ridge Press.

To find out more about the brain and the mind, try...

- Greenfield, Susan (Ed.) (1996). *The Human Mind Explained: An Owner's Guide to the Mysteries of the Mind.* New York, NY: Henry Holt Reference Book.
- Howard, Pierce (2000). *The Owner's Manual for the Brain: Everyday Applications from Mind-Brain Research.* Austin, TX: Bard Press.

For more exercises to improve the vision system, try...

- Richards, R. & Remick, K. (1988). *Classroom Visual Activities: A Manual to Embrace the Development of Visual Skills.* Novato, CA: Academic Therapy Publications.
- Remick, K., Stroud, C., & Bedes, V. (2000). *Eyes On Track: A Missing Link to Successful Learning.* Folsom, CA: JF's Publishing.
- Kimple, J. (1997). *Eye Q and the Efficient Learner.* Santa Ana, CA: Optometric Extension Program Foundation.

Other Related Readings From Corwin Press

10 Best Teaching Practice, 2nd Ed. (2005) by Donna Walker Tileston

12 Brain/Mind Learning Principles in Action (2005) by Renate Nummela Caine, Geoffrey Caine, Carol McClintic, and Karl Klimek

A Biological Brain in a Cultural Classroom, 2nd Ed. (2003) by Robert Sylvester

Becoming a "Wiz" at Brain-Based Teaching, 2nd Ed. (2006) by Marilee Sprenger

Brain-Based Learning, The Video Program for How the Brain Learns, Featuring David A. Sousa (2000)

Building the Reading Brain, PreK-3 (2004) by Patricia Wolfe and Pamela Nevills

Classroom Activators: 64 Novel Ways to Energize Learners (2004) by Jerry Evanski

Designing Brain-Compatible Learning, 3rd Ed. (2003) by Gayle Gregory and Terrence Parry

Environments for Learning (2003) by Eric Jensen

How the Brain Learns, 3rd Ed. (2006) by David A. Sousa

How the Brain Learns to Read (2005) by David A. Sousa

How the Brain Learns/Como Aprende el Cerebro, 2nd Ed./Segunda Edicion (2002) by David A. Sousa

How the Gifted Brain Learns (2003) by David A. Sousa

How the Special Needs Brain Learns (2001) by David A. Sousa

How to Explain a Brain (2005) by Robert Sylvester

Introduction to Brain-Compatible Learning (1998) by Eric Jensen

Learning Smarter (2001) by Eric Jensen and Michael Dabney

Learning with the Body in Mind (2000) by Eric Jensen

Mindful Learning (2003) by Linda Campbell

Music With the Brain in Mind (2000) by Eric Jensen

Sensorcises: Active Enrichment for the Out-of-Step Learner (2004) by Laurie Glazener

Sizzle and Substance (1998) by Eric Jensen

The Leadership Brain (2003) by David A. Sousa

Tools for Engagement (2003) by Eric Jensen

Trainer's Bonanza (1998) by Eric Jensen

TrainSmart: Perfect Trainings Every Time (2001) by Rich Allen

Bibliography

Ackerman, P., Holloway, C., Youngdahl, P., & Dykman, R. (2001). The double-deficit theory of reading disability does not fit all. *Learning Disabilities Research and Practice*, 16(3), 152–60.

Amen, Daniel (1998). *Change Your Brain, Change Your Life: The Breakthrough Program for Conquering Anxiety, Depression, Obsessiveness, Anger, and Impulsiveness.* New York, NY: Times Books/Random House.

Amen, Daniel (2002). *Healing the Hardware of the Soul: How Making the Brain-Soul Connection Can Optimize Your Life, Love, and Spiritual Growth.* New York, NY: The Free Press.

Antonietti, A. (1999). Can students predict when imagery will allow them to discover the problem solution? *European Journal of Cognitive Psychology*, 11(3), 407–28.

Antonietti, A., Cerana, P., & Scafidi, L. (1994). Mental visualization before and after problem presentation: A comparison. *Perceptual and Motor Skills*, 78(1), 179–89.

Auxter, D., Pyfer, J., & Huettig, C. (1996). *Adapted Physical Education and Recreation.* St. Louis, MO: Mosby.

Ball, W. & Blachman, B. (1991). Does phoneme awareness training in kindergarten make a difference in early work recognition and developmental spelling? *Reading Research Quarterly*, 26(1), 49–66.

Begley, Sharon (2002, October 11). Survival of the busiest: Parts of the brain that get most use literally expand and rewire. *The Wall Street Journal*, p. 1B.

Bernardi, L., Wdowczyk-Szulc, J., Valenti, C., Castoldi, S., Passino, C., Spadacini, G., & Sleight, P. (2000, May). Effects of controlled breathing, mental activity and mental stress with or without verbalization on heart rate variability. *Journal of the American College of Cardiology*, 35(6), 1462–9.

Binsted G., Chua, R., Helsen, W., & Elliott, D. (2001). Eye-hand coordination in goal-directed aiming. *Human Movement Science*, 20(4–5), 563–85.

Bjorklund, D. F. & Brown. R. D. (1998). Physical play and cognitive development: Integrating activity, cognition and education. *Child Development*, 69(3), 604–6.

Blaydes-Madigan, J. (2001). Advocacy: A case for daily quality physical education. Retrieved April 14, 2002, from Action Based Learning website: www.actionbasedlearning.com/cgi-bin/article.pl

Booth, J. R., Perfetti, C. A., & MacWhinney, B. (1999, Jan). Quick, automatic, and general activation of orthographic and phonological representations in young readers. *Developmental Psychology*, 35(1), 3–19.

Bower, G. H. & Mann, T. (1992). Improving recall by recoding interfering material at the time of retrieval. *Journal of Experimental Psychology: Learning, Memory, and Cognition*, 18(6), 1310–20.

Bower, G. H. & Morrow, G. (1990, Jan 5). Mental models in narrative comprehension. *Science*, 247(4938), 44–8.

Bower, James & Parsons, Lawrence (2003, August). Rethinking the "lesser brain." *Scientific American*, 289, 50–7.

Bransford, J., Brown, A., & Cocking, R. (Eds.) (2000). *How People Learn: Brain, Mind, Experience, and School—Expanded Edition.* Washington, DC: National Academy Press.

Brink, Susan (1995, May 15). Smart moves: New research suggests that folks from 8 to 80 can shape up their brains with aerobic exercise. *U.S. News & World Report*, 78–82.

Burgess, S. R. & Lonigan, C. J. (1998, Aug). Bidirectional relations of phonological sensitivity and prereading abilities: Evidence from a preschool sample. *Journal of Experimental Child Psychology*, 70(2), 117–41.

Cartwright, K. B. (2002). Cognitive development and reading: The relation of reading-specific multiple classification skill to reading comprehension in elementary school children. *Journal of Educational Psychology*, 94(1), 56–63.

Changeux, J. P. (1997, July). Variation and selection in neural function. *Trends in Neurosciences*, 20(7), 291–3.

Cheatum, B. & Hammond, A. (2000). *Physical Activities for Improving Children's Learning and Behavior: A Guide to Sensory Motor Development*. Champaign, IL: Human Kinetics.

Childre, Doc (1998). *Freeze Frame: A Scientifically Proven Technique for Clear Decision Making and Improved Health (2nd edition)*. Boulder Creek, CA: Planetary.

Cognitive Concepts, Inc.: Solutions for Literacy and Language. (1999). *The Research Basis of Earobics* [Brochure]. Evanston, IL.

Cool, Steven (1987). A view from the "outside": Sensory integration and developmental neurobiology. *Sensory Integration Special Interest Section Quarterly*, 10(2), 2–3.

Cool, Steven (2003, April 7). *Brain Plasticity and Physical Activities*. Springfield, OR: Paper presented at The First Annual Brain Center Conference, *The Brain: Understanding Neurology and Plasticity: Why Interventions Work!*

Crane, Adam & Soutar, Richard (2000). *Mindfitness Training: Neurofeedback and the Process*. San Jose, CA: Writers Club Press/iUniverse.

Cronin, V. S. (2002, Feb). The syntagmatic-paradigmatic shift and reading development. *Journal of Child Language*, 29(1), 189–204.

Dash, M. & Telles, S. (1999, Oct). Yoga training and motor speed based on a finger tapping task. *Indian Journal of Physiology and Pharmacology*, 43(4), 458–62.

Davis, Ronald & Braun, Eldon (1994). *The Gift of Dyslexia: Why Some of the Smartest People Can't Read and How They Can Learn*. New York, NY: Perigee Book.

De Quiros, J. B. (1976, Jan). Diagnosis of vestibular disorders in the learning disabled. *Journal of Learning Disabilities*, 9(1), 39–47.

Deal, Sheldon (1973). *Applied Kinesiology Workshop Manual*. New Life Publishing Co.

Diamond, Marian & Hopson, Janet (1999). *Magic Trees of the Mind: How to Nurture Your Child's Intelligence, Creativity, and Healthy Emotions from Birth through Adolescence*. New York, NY: Plume.

Diorio, D., Viau, V., & Meaney, M. (1993, Sept). The role of the medial prefrontal cortex (cingulate gyrus) in the regulation of hypothalamic-pituitary-adrenal responses to stress. *Journal of Neuroscience*, 13(9), 3839–47.

Dobie, T. G., May, J. G., Gutierrez, C., & Heller, S. S. (1990, Dec). The transfer of adaptation between actual and simulated rotary stimulation. *Aviation, Space, and Environmental Medicine*, 61(12), 1085–91.

Dooley, K. O. & Farmer, A. (1988, Aug). Comparison for aphasic and control subjects of eye movements hypothesized in neurolinguistic programming. *Perceptual and Motor Skills*, 67(1), 233–4.

Drake, Susan (1996). Guided imagery and education: Theory, practice and experience. *Journal of Mental Imagery*, 20(1), 1–58.

Eden, G. F. & Moats, L. (2002, Nov). The role of neuroscience in the remediation of students with dyslexia. *Nature Neuroscience,* Supplement 5, 1080–4.

Fast ForWord: High-tech help for language learning impairments. (1998, Spring). *Curriculum•Technology Quarterly*, 7(2).

Fast ForWord: A Review. (2002, May 21). Retrieved September 4, 2003, from the Education Commission of the States website: www.ecs.org/clearinghouse/18/84/1884.htm

Fawcett, A., Nicolson, R., & Dean, P. (1996). Impaired performance of children with dyslexia on a range of cerebellar tests. *Annals of Dyslexia*, 46, 259–83.

Frank, J. & Levinson, H. (1973, Oct). Dysmetric dyslexia and dyspraxia: Hypothesis and study. *Journal of the American Academy of Child Psychiatry*, 12(4), 690–701.

Fuchs, D., Fuchs, L., Mathes, P., Lipsey, M., & Roberts, P. (2001, August). *Is "Learning Disabilities" Just a Fancy Term for Low Achievement? A Meta-Analysis of Reading Differences between Low Achievers with and without the Label*. Washington, DC: Paper presented at *The Learning Disabilities Summit: Building a Foundation for the Future*.

Furr, David (2000). *Reading Clinic: Brain Research Applied to Reading*. Chicago, IL: Truman House Publishing.

Gabbard, C. (1998). Windows of opportunity for early brain and motor development. *Journal of Physical Education, Recreation, and Dance*, 69(8), 54–61.

Gardner, Howard (1999). *Intelligence Reframed: Multiple Intelligences for the 21st Century*. New York, NY: Basic Books.

Genesee, F. (2000). Brain research: Implications for second language learning (Report No. EDO-FL-00-12). Washington, DC: Office of Educational Research and Improvement. (ERIC Document Reproduction Service No. 447727)

Gerlic, I. & Jausovec, N. (1999). Multimedia: Differences in cognitive processes observed with EEG. *Educational Technology Research and Development*, 47(3), 5–14.

Gilbert, Anne Green (1977). *Teaching the Three Rs through Movement Experiences: A Handbook for Teachers*. New York: Burgess.

Goddard, Sally (2002). *Reflexes, Learning and Behavior: A Window into the Child's Mind*. Eugene, OR: Fern Ridge Press.

Goddard, Sally (1996). *A Teacher's Window into the Child's Mind and Papers from the Institute for Neuro-Physiological Psychology*. Eugene, OR: Fern Ridge Press.

Gold, S. (2002). Exercises to help your child: Therapy for behavior problems, learning problems, ADD and autism. Retrieved June 20, 2002, from Fern Ridge Press website: www.fernridgepress.com/autism.exercise.phases.html

Goswami, U. (1993). Toward an interactive analogy model of reading development: Vowel graphemes in beginning reading. *Journal of Experimental Student Psychology*, 54, 443–75.

Graham, S., Berninger, V., Weintraub, N., & Schafer, W. (1998). Development of handwriting speed and legibility in grades 1–9. *The Journal of Educational Research*, 92(1), 42–52.

Graham S., Harris, K., & Fink, B. (2000). Is handwriting causally related to learning to write? Treatment of handwriting problems in beginning writers. *Journal of Educational Psychology*, 92(4), 620–33.

Greenfield, Susan (Ed.) (1996). *The Human Mind Explained: An Owner's Guide to the Mysteries of the Mind*. New York, NY: Henry Holt Reference Book.

Griffin, M. J. & Brett, M. W. (1997, Dec). Effects of fore-and-aft, lateral and vertical whole-body vibration on a head-positioning task. *Aviation, Space, and Environmental Medicine*, 68(12), 1115–22.

Gurian, Michael (2001). *Boys and Girls Learn Differently!: A Guide for Teachers and Parents*. San Francisco, CA: Jossey-Bass.

Hannaford, Carla (2002). *Awakening the Child Heart*. Captain Cook, HI: Jamilla Nur Publishing.

Hannaford, Carla (1995). *Smart Moves: Why Learning is Not All in Your Head*. Arlington, VA: Great Ocean Publishers.

Haybach, P. J. (2001, Jan. 12). Preventing balance and hearing problems. Retrieved November 7, 2002, from Vestibular Disorders Association website: www.vestibular.org/prevent.html

Healy, Jane (1994). *Your Child's Growing Mind: A Guide to Learning and Brain Development from Birth to Adolescence*. New York, NY: Main Street Books.

Henning, R. A., Jacques, P., Kissel, G. V., Sullivan, A. B., & Alteras-Webb, S. M. (1997, Jan). Frequent short rest breaks for computer work: Effects on productivity and well-being at two field sites. *Ergonomics*, 40(1), 78–91.

Houde, O. (2000). Inhibition and cognitive development: Object, number, categorization, and reasoning. *Cognitive Development*, 15(1), 63–73.

Howard, Pierce (2000). The body cognitive: The effects of exercise. In, *The Owner's Manual for the Brain: Everyday Applications from Mind-Brain Research*. Austin, TX: Bard Press.

Jensen, Eric (2000a). *Brain-Based Learning (Revised)*. Thousand Oaks, CA: Corwin Press.

Jensen, Eric (1997). *Completing the Puzzle: The Brain-Compatible Approach to Learning (2nd Edition)*. Thousand Oaks, CA: Corwin Press.

Jensen, Eric (2000b). *Learning with the Body in Mind*. Thousand Oaks, CA: Corwin Press.

Jensen, Eric & Dabney, Michael (2000). *Learning Smarter: The New Science of Teaching.* Thousand Oaks, CA: Corwin Press.

Johnson R., Nottingham, D., Stratton, R., & Zaba, J. (1996). The vision screening of academically and behaviorally at-risk pupils. *Journal of Behavioral Optometry,* 7(2), 39–42.

Jones, D. & Christensen, C. (1999). Relationship between automaticity in handwriting and student's ability to generate written text. *Journal of Educational Psychology,* 91(1), 44–9.

Kempermann, G. & Gage, F. (1999, May). New nerve cells for the adult brain. *Scientific American,* 280(5), 48–53.

Kermoian, R. & Campos, J. J. (1988, Aug). Locomotor experience: A facilitator of spatial cognitive development. *Child Development,* 59(4), 908–17.

Khalsa, G. & Sifft, J. (1987). *The Effects of Educational Kinesiology upon the Static Balance of Learning Disabled Boys and Girls.* Las Vegas, NV: Paper presented at the National Convention of the American Alliance for Health, Physical Education, Recreation, and Dance. (ERIC Document Reproduction Service No. ED289835)

Kimple, J. (1997). *Eye Q and the Efficient Learner.* Santa Ana, CA: Optometric Extension Program Foundation.

Koslowe, K. C. (1995). Optometric services in a reading disability clinic: Initial results. *Journal of Behavioral Optometry,* 6(3), 67–8.

Kranowitz, C. S. (2003). *The Out-of-Sync Child Has Fun: Activities for Kids with Sensory Integration Dysfunction.* New York, NY: Perigee.

Kranowitz, C. S. & Szklut, S. (2000). *Teachers Ask About Sensory Integration: Companion Booklet for Audio Media.* Boulder, CO: Bell Curve Records.

Kujala, T., Karma, K., Ceponiene, R., Belitz, S., Turkkila, P., Tervaniemi, M., & Naatanen, R. (2001, Aug 28). Plastic neural changes and reading improvement caused by audio-visual training in reading-impaired children. *Proceedings of the National Academy of Sciences (USA),* 98(18), 10509–14.

Lacey, B. C. & Lacey, J. I. (1978, Feb). Two-way communication between the heart and the brain. Significance of time within the cardiac cycle. *American Psychologist,* 33(2), 99–113.

LeDoux, J. (1996). *The Emotional Brain.* New York: Simon & Schuster.

Lefebvre, C. & Reid, G. (1998). Prediction in ball catching by children with and without a developmental coordination disorder. *Adapted Physical Activity Quarterly,* 15(4), 299–315.

Levine, Mel (1999). Acquiring motor mastery. Retrieved September 17, 2002, from All Kinds of Minds website: www.allkindsofminds.org/learningBaseCategory.aspx?categoryID=5

Levine, Mel (1990). *Keeping a Head in School: A Student's Book about Learning Abilities and Learning Disorders.* Cambridge, MA: Educators Publishing Services.

Levine, Mel (2003). *A Mind at a Time.* New York, NY: Simon & Schuster.

Levinson, H. (2002). Medical Treatment. Retrieved November 7, 2002, from the Levinson Medical Center for Learning Disabilities website: www.dyslexiaonline.com/information/treatment.html

Long, D., Oppy, D., & Seely, M. (1997). Individual differences in readers' sentence- and text-level representation. *Journal of Memory and Language,* 36(1), 129–45.

Maguire, J. (1996). *Become Pain-Free with Touch For Health.* Malibu, CA: Kinesiology Institute.

Mahony, D., Singson, M., & Mann, V. (2000). Reading ability and sensitivity to morphological relations. *Reading and Writing: An Interdisciplinary Journal,* 12(3), 191–218.

Marzano, R., Pickering, D., & Pollock, J. (2001). *Classroom Instruction that Works: Research-Based Strategies for Increasing Student Achievement.* Alexandria, VA: Association for Supervision and Curriculum Development.

Marsiglia, Susan (2002, August 2). Children's reading disability attributed to brain impairment. Retrieved September 3, 2003, from National Institutes of Health website: www.nih.gov/news/pr/aug2002/nichd-02.htm

McCraty, R, Atkinson, M., Tiller, W. A., Rein, G., & Watkins, A. D. (1995, Nov). The effects of emotions on short-term power spectrum analysis of heart rate variability. *American Journal of Cardiology*, 76(14), 1089–93.

McCraty, R., Atkinson, M., & Tomasino, D. (2001). *Science of the Heart: Exploring the Role of the Heart in Human Performance—An Overview of Research Conducted by the Institute of HeartMath* (Publication No. 01-001). Boulder Creek, CO: Institute of HeartMath.

Meschyan, G. & Hernandez, A. E. (2002). Is native language decoding skill related to second language learning? *Journal of Educational Psychology*, 94(1), 14–22.

Metzer, D. & Schur, D. (1967). *Suppression, Academic Performance and Near Optometric Findings: A Correlation Study*. Unpublished doctoral thesis, Pacific University, Forest Grove, Oregon.

Mon-Williams, M., Tresilian, J., & Wann, J. (1999, June). Perceiving limb position in normal and abnormal control: An equilibrium point perspective. *Human Movement Science*, 18, 397–419.

Murphy, M. & Donovan, S. (1988). *The Physical and Psychological Effects of Meditation*. San Rafael, CA: Esalen Institute.

Mushiake, H. & Strick, P. L. (1995, Dec). Pallidal neuron activity during sequential arm movements. *Journal of Neurophysiology*, 74(6), 2754–8.

Nation, K. & Snowling, M. (1998, July). Semantic processing and the development of word recognition skills: Evidence from children with reading comprehension difficulties. *Journal of Memory and Language*, 39(1), 85–101.

O'Keefe, J. & Nadel, L. (1978). *The Hippocampus as a Cognitive Map*. New York, NY: Clarendon Press.

Omi, S. (1998). *Fifty Years of the World Health Organization in the Western Pacific Region: Report of the Regional Director to the Regional Committee for the Western Pacific (Vol. 2)*. Manila: World Health Organization (Western Pacific Region).

Paivio, A. (1971). *Imagery and Verbal Processes*. New York, NY: Holt, Rinehard & Winston.

Paivio, A. (1969). Mental imagery in associative learning and memory. *Psychological Review*, 76(3), 241–63.

Paivio, A. (1990). *Mental Representations: A Dual Coding Approach*. New York, NY: Oxford University Press.

Palmer, L. (1980). Auditory discrimination development through vestibulo-cochlear stimulation. *Academic Therapy*, 16(1), 55–68.

Peer, Lindsay (2002). Research reviews. Retrieved June 12, 2002, from the British Dyslexia Association website: www.bda-dyslexia.org.uk/main/research/doc/Research_Reviews_Part1_and_Part2.pdf

Pokorni, J. L. & Jamison, P. J. (1999) *A Comparison of Three Programs: Fast ForWord, Earobics, and LiPS—A Steppingstones Project*. [PowerPoint Presentation]. Co-Sponsored by Pacific Institute for Research and Evaluation (Calverton, MD) and Prince George's County Public Schools (Upper Marlboro, MD).

Post, Y. V., Foorman, B. R., & Hiscock, M. (1997). Speech perception and speech production as indicators of reading difficulty. *Annals of Dyslexia*, 47(1), 3–27.

Promislow, Sharon (2000). *Making the Brain/Body Connection: A Playful Guide to Releasing Mental, Physical and Emotional Blocks to Stress*. West Vancouver, BC: Kinetic Publishing.

Prothero, J. D., Draper, M. H., Furness, T. A., Parker, D. E., & Wells, M. J. (1999, Mar). The use of an independent visual background to reduce simulator side-effects. *Aviation, Space and Environmental Medicine*, 70(3 Pt 1), 277–83.

Rapp, D. N. & Samuel, A. G. (2002, May). A reason to rhyme: Phonological and semantic influences on lexical access. *Journal of Experimental Psychology: Learning, Memory, and Cognition*, 28(3), 564–71.

Rein, G., Atkinson, M., & McCraty, R. (1995). The physiological and psychological effects of compassion and anger. *Journal of Advancement in Medicine*, 8(2), 87–105.

Remick, K., Stroud, C., & Bedes, V. (2000). *Eyes on Track: A Missing Link to Successful Learning*. Folsom, CA: JF's Publishing.

Reschke, M. F., Bloomberg, J. J., Harm, D. L., Paloski, W. H., Layne, C. C., & McDonald, V. (1998). Posture, locomotion, spatial orientation, and motion sickness as a function of space flights. *Brain Research Reviews*, 28(1–2), 102–17.

Restak, Richard (1995). *Brainscapes: An Introduction to What Neuroscience Has Learned about the Structure, Function, and Abilities of the Brain*. New York, NY: Hyperion.

Riccio, C. A., Hynd, G. W., Cohen, M. J., Hall, J., & Molt, L. (1994). Comorbidity of central auditory processing disorder and attention-deficit hyperactivity disorder. *Journal of the American Academy of Child and Adolescent Psychiatry*, 33(6), 849–57.

Richards, R. & Remick, K. (1988). *Classroom Visual Activities (CVA): A Manual to Enhance the Development of Visual Skills*. Novato, CA: Academic Therapy Publications.

Richardson, A. (1983). Imagery: Definitions and types. In A. A. Sheikh (Ed.), *Imagery: Current Theory, Research, and Application* (pp. 3–42). New York, NY: John Wiley & Sons.

Riehle, A., Kornblum, S., & Requin, J. (1997, Dec). Neuronal correlates of sensorimotor association in stimulus-response compatibility. *Journal of Experimental Psychology. Human Perception and Performance*, 23(6), 1708–26.

Robbins, Jim (2000). *A Symphony in the Brain: The Evolution of the New Brain Wave Biofeedback*. New York: Grove Press.

Russell, Peter (1979). *The Brain Book* (pp. 186–210). New York, NY: Plume.

Sapolsky, R. M. (1999, March). Stress and your brain: Trauma survivors can lose more than peace of mind. They may also lose some gray matter. *Discover*, 116.

Sapolsky, R. M. (1996, Aug 9). Why stress is bad for your brain. *Science*, 273(5276), 749–50.

Schacter, J. (2000). *Reading Programs that Work: A Review of Programs for Pre-Kindergarten to 4th Grade*. Santa Monica, CA: Milken Family Foundation.

Schminky, M. & Baran, J. (1999). Central auditory processing disorders: An overview of assessment and management practices. *Deaf-Blind Perspectives*, 7(1), 1–7.

Schneider, C. C. (2001). *Sensory Secrets: How to Jump-Start Learning in Children*. Siloam Springs, AR: Concerned Communications.

Schoemaker, M. M., Van Der Wees, M., Flapper, B., Verheij-Jansen, N., Scholten-Jaegers, S., & Geuze, R. (2001, Mar). Perceptual skills of children with developmental coordination disorder. *Human Movement Science*, 20(1–2), 111–33.

The Scientific American Book of the Brain. (1999). New York, NY: The Lyons Press.

Secades, F. (1984). When does the child climb the stairs? *Psicologica* (University of Valencia, Spain), 5(3), 241–263.

Shannahoff-Khalsa, D. (1983, January 3). Breathing cycle linked to hemispheric dominance. *Brain Mind Bulletin*, 8(3).

Sifft, J. M. (1990). *Education Kinesiology: Empowering Students and Athletes through Movement*. New Orleans, LA: Paper presented at the 57th National Convention of the American Alliance for Health, Physical Education, Recreation, and Dance (ERIC Document Reproduction Service No. ED320891).

Smits-Engelsman, B. C., Niemeijer, A. S., & Van Galen, G. P. (2001, Mar). Fine motor deficiencies in children diagnosed as DCD based on poor grapho-motor ability. *Human Movement Science*, 20(1–2), 161–82.

Smits-Engelsman, B. C. & Van Galen, G. P. (1997, Nov). Dysgraphia in children: Lasting psychomotor deficiency or transient developmental delay? *Journal of Experimental Child Psychology*, 67(2), 164–84.

Spache, G., Hinds, L., & Bing, L. (1992). *Vision and School Success: A Guide to Understanding Vision's Role in Learning and What the Teacher Can Do to Facilitate Learning in the Classroom*. Santa Ana, CA: VisionExtension.

Stables, K. (1997). Critical issues to consider when introducing technology education into the curriculum of young learners. *Journal of Technology Education*, 8(2), 50–65.

Sunbeck, Deborah (1996). *Infinity Walk: Preparing Your Mind to Learn! (2nd Edition)*. Torrance, CA: Jalmar Press.

Sylwester, Robert (2000). *A Biological Brain in a Cultural Classroom: Applying Biological Research to Classroom Management*. Thousand Oaks, CA: Corwin Press.

Sylwester, Robert (1995). *A Celebration of Neurons: An Educator's Guide to the Human Brain*. Alexandria, VA: Association for Supervision and Curriculum Development.

Temple, E., Poldrack, R. A., Protopapas, A., Nagarajan, S., Salz, T., Tallal, P., & Merzenich, M. M. (2000, Dec). Disruption of the neural response to rapid acoustic stimuli in dyslexia: Evidence from functional MRI. *Proceedings from the National Academy of the Sciences (USA)*, 97(25), 13907–12.

Topping, W. (1990). *Success Over Distress: Using Muscle Testing to Help You Master Your Fears, to Expand Your Awareness, and Reach Your Full Potential*. Bellingham, WA: Topping International Institute.

Torgesen, J. K. (2001). *Empirical and Theoretical Support for Direct Diagnosis of Learning Disabilities by Assessment of Intrinsic Processing Weaknesses*. Washington, DC: Paper presented at *Learning Disabilities Summit: Building a Foundation for the Future* (August 27–28, 2001).

Torgesen, J. K., Rashotte, C., Alexander, A., Alexander, J., & MacPhee, K. (2003). Progress toward understanding the instructional conditions necessary for remediating reading difficulties in older children. In B. Foormand (Ed.), *Preventing and Remediating Reading Difficulties: Bringing Science to Scale*. Timonium, MD: York Press.

Torgesen, J. K., Wagner, R. K., Balthazar, M., Davis, C., Morgan, S., Simmons, K., Stage, S., & Zirps, F. (1989, June). Developmental and individual differences in performance on phonological synthesis tasks. *Journal of Experimental Child Psychology*, 47(3), 491–505.

Tortora, Gerard J. & Anagnostakos, Nicholas P. (1990). *Principles of Anatomy and Physiology (6th edition)*. New York, NY: HarperCollins.

Travis, F. (1998, May). Cortical and cognitive development in 4th, 8th and 12th grade students: The contribution of speed of processing and executive functioning to cognitive development. *Biological Psychology*, 48(1), 37–56.

Van Galen, G. P., Portier, S. J., Smits-Engelsman, B. C. M., & Schomaker, L. R. B. (1993, Mar). Neuromotor noise and poor handwriting in children. *Acta Pschologica*, 82, 161–78.

Vogel, G. (1995). Saccadic eye movements: Theory, testing and therapy. *Journal of Behavioral Optometry*, 6(1), 3–12.

Willette T. L. & Early, G. H. (1985, Dec). Abilities of normal and reading-disabled children to combine the visual and auditory modalities with dimensions of space and time. *Perceptual and Motor Skills*, 61(3 Pt 2), 1295–8.

Willoughby, T., Desmarais, S., Wood, E., Sims, S., & Kalra, M. (1997, Dec). Mechanisms that facilitate the effectiveness of elaboration strategies. *Journal of Educational Psychology*, 89(4), 682–5.

Winebrenner, Susan (1996). *Teaching Kids with Learning Difficulties in the Regular Classroom: Strategies and Techniques Every Teacher Can Use to Challenge and Motivate Struggling Students*. Minneapolis, MN: Free Spirit Publishing.

Wise, Anna (1995). *The High-Performance Mind: Mastering Brainwaves for Insight, Healing, and Creativity*. New York, NY: J. P. Tarcher.

Woodman, P. D. & Griffin, M. J. (1997, Feb). Effect of direction of head movement on motion sickness caused by Coriolis stimulation. *Aviation, Space, and Environmental Medicine*, 68(2), 93–8.

Yan, J. H., Thomas, J. R., & Downing, J. H. (1998, Aug). Locomotion improves children's spatial search: A meta-analytic review. *Perceptual Motor Skills*, 87(1), 67–82.

Yopp, H. K. (1988, Spring). The validity and reliability of phonemic awareness tests. *Reading Research Quarterly*, 23, 159–77.

Zametkin, A. J. (1995, June 21). Attention deficit disorder: Born to be hyperactive? *Journal of the American Medical Association*, 273(23), 1871–4.

Index